# Furniture of Pine, Poplar, and Maple

# FURNITURE *of*
## *Pine, Poplar, and Maple*

FRANKLIN H. GOTTSHALL

BONANZA BOOKS · NEW YORK

# Preface

Plain and simple things often have a great deal of beauty. This truth applies not only to the fine arts, but also to other fields of creativity in which art principles are used to achieve beauty. The principle is particularly applicable in the designing of furniture.

In this new book of furniture designs, the author has endeavored to simplify lines and surfaces, and to hold ornament to a minimum. Simple outline, good proportion, sound construction, the use of materials of good quality, have been adhered to in the design of the thirty-five pieces of furniture which are presented here. In place of ornament, the natural beauty of wood has been exploited. Even turning has been held to a minimum in the design of these projects, and where turnings have been used, they have been kept as simple as possible.

None of the designs presented here are beyond the capabilities of high school students, and certainly not beyond the capabilities of a considerable number of home workshop enthusiasts.

Whenever the author felt there was the least likelihood that construction details might not be clearly understood by an examination of the orthographic drawings, additional helps were added, such as detailed drawings, exploded views, photographs, sketches, and written instructions in the text.

The designs have not been limited to traditional styles: a number approach what would now be accepted as Contemporary. In all of them, usefulness and function have played an important part in determining what should be included in this book. The achievement of variety in design, the use to which the design was to be put, and the services it was to perform were carefully considered.

The author hopes he has in large measure succeeded in the task he set for himself when this work was begun: to try to present to his many friends and to users of previously published books on furniture design some new and worthwhile pieces they will find to their liking, and will, therefore, wish to build.

FRANKLIN H. GOTTSHALL

This edition published by Bonanza Books
a division of Crown Publishers, Inc.,
by arrangement with the author.

(C)

# Contents

# 1. Welsh Dresser

Fig. 1

One of the best places to display fine china, pewter, or highly prized bric-a-brac, is in an open Welsh dresser like the one shown in Figure 1 (which belongs to the author). Such a dresser may also serve as a bookcase in a library or den. Despite the size of this piece, it is quite simple to build. The lines of the design are straight, making it easy to get out stock, to plane, sand, and assemble the piece, once everything is ready. The great amount of storage space provided by the large, sturdy drawers makes this a very desirable piece to own.

Start building the Welsh Dresser by first gluing up boards for the ends (A). A full-sized pattern for these may be made by drawing 2-in. graph squares, as shown in Figure 3. Next, glue up the table board. Then glue up the partitions (E).

11

# Welsh Dresser

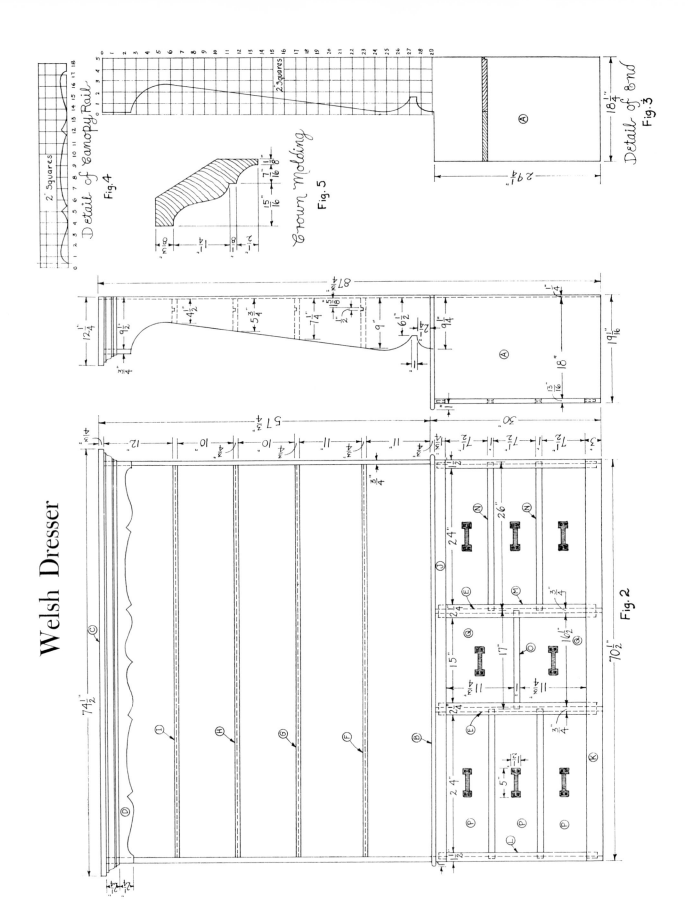

Detail of Canopy Rail  Fig.4

2" Squares

2 3 squares

Crown Molding  Fig.5

$\frac{7}{16}$"  $\frac{11}{8}$"
$\frac{15}{16}$"
$\frac{3}{8}$"  $1\frac{1}{4}$"  $\frac{1}{8}$"  2"

Detail of End  Fig.3

$18\frac{1}{4}$"  $29\frac{1}{4}$"

Ⓐ

Fig.2

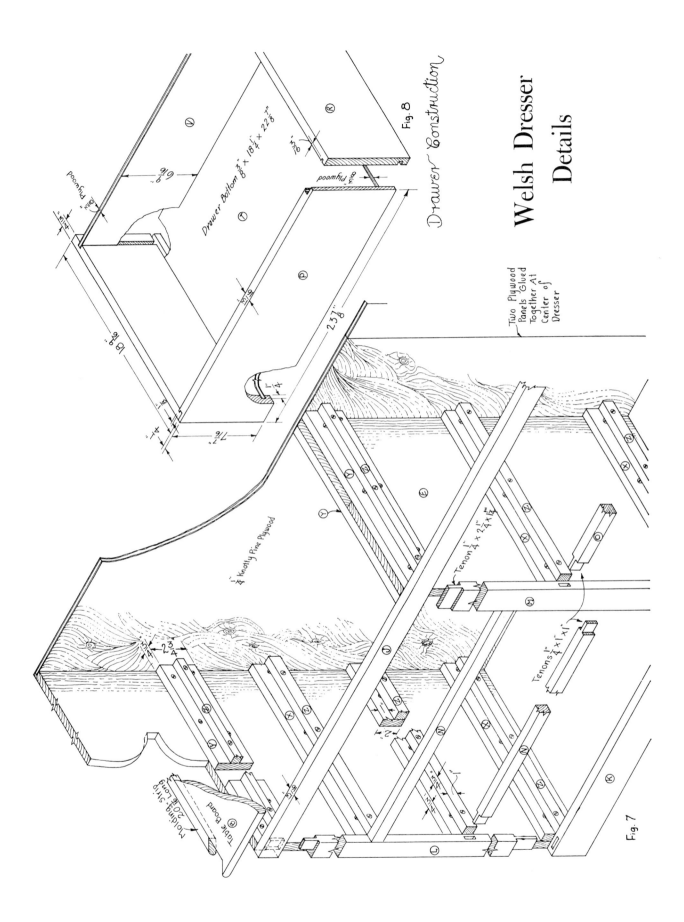

Welsh Dresser
Details

Fig. 8

Drawer Construction

Drawer Bottom ⅜" × 18¼" × 22⅞"

9½"

18⅞"

⅛" plywood

¾" plywood

¾" plywood

3⅛"

¼"

7⅜"

23⅞"

Two Plywood Panels Glued Together At Center of Dresser

¾" Knotty Pine Plywood

2¾"

Tenon ¼" × 2¼" × 1¼"

Tenons ¼" × 1" × 1"

Molding 5' long
2'0" long
Table Board

Fig. 7

13

Get out stock for the frame, which is nailed to the front. Cut the mortises and tenons on the rails and stiles, and glue the pieces together, as shown in Figures 2 and 7. The stiles (*L*) and (*M*), and the short rails (*N*) and (*O*) must be joined together before the long rails are joined to them.

Rabbet the rear edges of the ends (*A*). Lay out lines marking the locations of the drawer guides (*X*) and (*Y*) on the inside of each end and on both sides of the partitions. Saw these out and screw them fast. Then saw out and screw fast the drawer runs.

You are now ready to begin assembling the parts you have made. First nail the frame to the ends, using 6-penny finishing nails. Then nail the partitions to the frame. Check to see that all drawer runs are perfectly square with the front of the cabinet, and level on top, with the rails. Then nail on the table-board. Cut out and nail on the molding strips at the ends of the table-board.

Cut and nail the shelves in place. Notice that each shelf has a plate groove cut 1⅝ in. from the rear edge (End view, Fig. 2). Saw and nail on the canopy board, and then the top. Make or buy the crown molding, and nail it fast.

In fastening the back, note that it is composed of two panels, which should be glued together where they are joined in the middle of the dresser. Glue may be put on this joint when the second panel is being nailed to the back, provided the adjoining edges fit each other perfectly.

All that now remains to be done is to make the drawers. The drawer sides are intentionally made extra heavy, so that they will be strong enough to hold heavy loads. A rugged, machine-made drawer joint (Fig. 8) is used here. Dovetailed joints would be better, and perhaps even more appropriate than those which are shown. The ones shown in Figure 8 are as strong, however, when glued and nailed together as dovetail joints would be.

The finish used on this piece of furniture is the same as that recommended for the Trestle Table, described on page 20.

## BILL OF MATERIAL

| DESCRIPTION | PIECES | DIMENSIONS |
|---|---|---|
| Ends (A) | 2 | ¾ x 18¼ x 87 |
| Table board (B) | 1 | ¾ x 19 13/16 x 72½ |
| Top (C) | 1 | ¾ x 12¼ x 74½ |
| Canopy board (D) | 1 | ¾ x 4½ x 70½ |
| Partitions (E) | 2 | ¾ x 18 x 29¼ |
| Lower shelf (F) | 1 | ¾ x 9 x 69 |
| Second shelf (G) | 1 | ¾ x 7¼ x 69 |
| Third shelf (H) | 1 | ¾ x 5¾ x 69 |
| Upper shelf (I) | 1 | ¾ x 4½ x 69 |
| Upper rail (J) | 1 | 13/16 x 1¾ x 70½ |
| Lower rail (K) | 1 | 13/16 x 3 x 70½ |
| Stiles (L) | 2 | 13/16 x 1½ x 27¾ |
| Stiles (M) | 2 | 13/16 x 2¼ x 27¾ |
| Rails (N) | 4 | 13/16 x 1 x 26 |
| Rail (O) | 1 | 13/16 x 1 x 17 |
| Drawer fronts (P) | 6 | 13/16 x 7 7/16 x 23⅞ |
| Drawer fronts (Q) | 2 | 13/16 x 11 11/16 x 14⅞ |
| Drawer sides (R) | 12 | ¾ x 7 7/16 x 18 9/16 |
| Drawer sides (S) | 4 | ¾ x 11 11/16 x 18 9/16 |
| Drawer bottoms (T) | 6 | plywood ⅜ x 18¼ x 22⅞ |
| Drawer bottoms (U) | 2 | plywood ⅜ x 18¼ x 13⅞ |
| Drawer backs (V) | 6 | plywood ⅜ x 6 9/16 x 22⅞ |
| Drawer backs (W) | 2 | plywood ⅜ x 10 13/16 x 13⅞ |
| Drawer guides (X) | 16 | ¾ x 2 x 18 |
| Drawer guides (Y) | 4 | ¾ x 2¾ x 18 |
| Drawer runs (Z) | 22 | ¾ x 1 x 18 |
| Back of cabinet | 2 | knotty pine plywood ¼ x 34⅞ x 87¾ |
| Crown molding | 1 | 9 ft. |
| Molding strips | 2 | ¾ x 1 x 20 1/16 |

Fig. 9

The deep, wide corner cupboard shown in Figure 9 is a featured piece in a new living room which the author recently added to his home. Few other woods possess the quaint charm of knotty white pine, which turns a warm and satisfying yellow hue when given a natural finish. Double glass doors could be added to this cupboard, if desired. The hand-carved shell, not shown in the drawings, was added after the cupboard had been built, and its inclusion is optional.

Ceiling height will determine the height of a piece of furniture such as this, which may easily

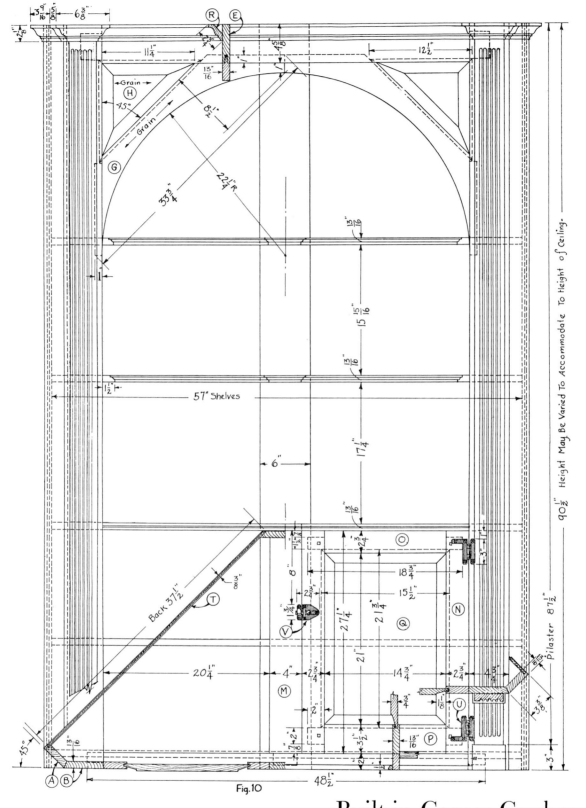

Fig. 10

## Built-in Corner Cupboard

16

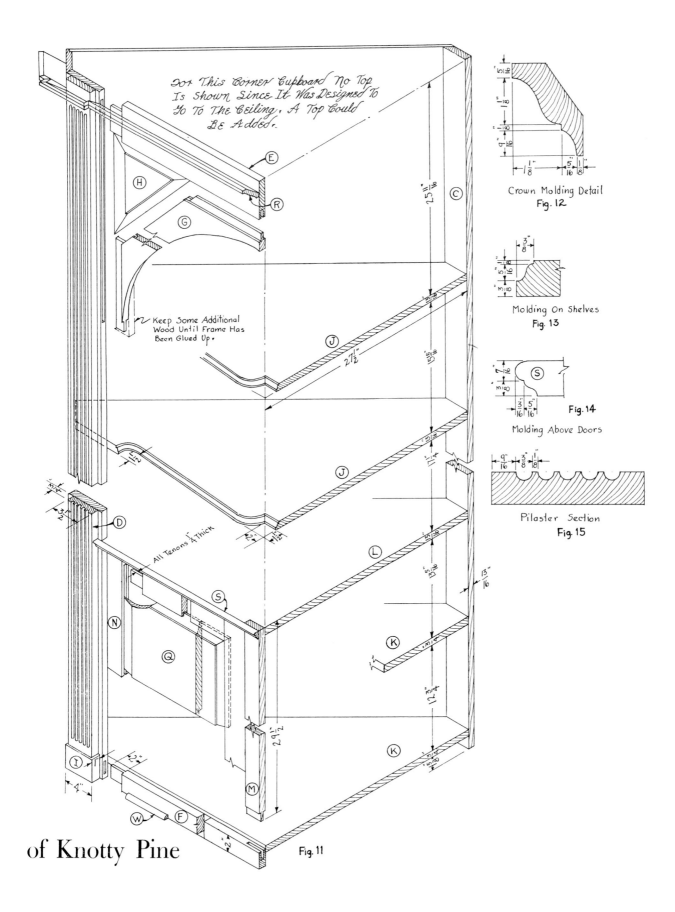

For This Corner Cupboard No Top Is Shown Since It Was Designed To Go To The Ceiling. A Top Could Be Added.

E

H

R

G

Keep Some Additional Wood Until Frame Has Been Glued Up.

C

J

$27\frac{1}{2}$"

$25\frac{11}{16}$"

$15\frac{5}{16}$"

$1\frac{1}{2}$"

J

$17\frac{1}{4}$"

All Tenons $\frac{1}{4}$ Thick

$1\frac{1}{2}$

D

S

L

$15\frac{5}{16}$"

N

Q

K

$29\frac{1}{2}$"

$12\frac{3}{4}$"

$\frac{13}{16}$"

K

I

$4$"

M

$2$"

W    F

of Knotty Pine

Fig. 11

Crown Molding Detail
Fig. 12

$\frac{3}{8}$"

Molding On Shelves
Fig. 13

S

Fig. 14

Molding Above Doors

$\frac{9}{16}$"  $\frac{3}{8}$"  $\frac{1}{8}$"

Pilaster Section
Fig. 15

be adapted to that of any room, though the height of the top of the table shelf is about as it should be regardless of changes which may have to be made on the upper part. Spacing of the shelves is also optional.

As shown in Figures 10 and 11, the construction is not very difficult. For anyone with woodworking machinery, the making of this piece should pose few difficulties.

To build the corner cupboard, first make the frame for the front. Its width will determine both the width and depth of the cupboard. First saw the stiles (*B*) and posts (*A*) to their proper widths, then plane and sand them. Lay out mortises on the stiles to which rails (*E*) and (*F*) will be joined, and also the grooves at the top into which the triangular-shaped panels are to be fitted. Cut the mortises.

Next, make the cross rails (*E*) and (*F*) and the arched rails (*G*). Cut grooves and mortises into these, as shown at the top of Figure 11. Cut and fit the tenons, and make a trial assembly of these parts.

Cut and raise the panels. Panel raising may be done by tilting the circular saw to the proper angle (about 15 deg.) and running the panels through vertically. (Panel raising is shown being done on the wastebasket panels [Fig. 34].) Saw marks will have to be scraped off and sanded, but this job does not take long.

When you have everything fitting properly, glue the frame together. The stile (*M*) between the lower doors may be made and glued on after the shelves and frame have been assembled.

Cut the outside edges of the stiles to an angle of 70 deg. Cut the edge of the post, which is to be joined to the stile, to an angle of 65 deg. Thus the posts may be fitted to the stiles so they will be at an angle of 90 deg. with the wall against which the corner cupboard is placed.

On this corner cupboard the posts and stiles were glued and nailed together with 4-penny finishing nails. A rabbet cut along the back edges of the posts will allow the plywood back to be nailed fast so the edge of the plywood will not show. This plywood is not nailed on until all shelves have been fastened to the front and to the rear post. The upper shelves must be sawed to shape and molded on the front edges before being nailed in place.

If a corner cupboard is to be fitted properly to a plastered wall, which may not be altogether plumb or straight, the rabbets on the rear of the corner posts may have to be cut deeper than 3/8 in. to allow room for scribing the edge so it may be fitted to the wall properly. This would make a slight difference in the size of the shelves from that which is given in the bill of material.

Once the shelves, the front, and the rear post have been assembled, the plywood backs may be nailed fast.

The fluted pilasters should be made next. The flutes on these may very easily be cut by using a power hand router, but on this cupboard they were cut by hand with a wood carver's fluting chisel. Nail these to the cupboard leaving the proper width on the inside of the stile to fasten the H-L hinge. Make and nail on the base blocks.

One of the more difficult tasks in making this cupboard is to fit the pieces of crown molding where they go around the pilaster. Three of these pieces must be cut very short, and it is no easy matter to assemble and fasten them properly (see the detail at top of Fig. 11).

The doors are made next. Make the stiles, mor-

**BILL OF MATERIAL**

| DESCRIPTION | PIECES | DIMENSIONS |
|---|---|---|
| End posts (A) | 2 | 13/16 x 3 3/8 x 90 1/2 |
| Stiles on frame (B) | 2 | 13/16 x 4 3/4 x 90 1/2 |
| Rear post (C) | 1 | 13/16 x 6 x 90 1/2 |
| Pilasters (D) | 2 | 3/4 x 3 1/2 x 87 1/2 |
| Top rail (E) | 1 | 13/16 x 4 5/8 x 48 1/2 |
| Bottom rail (F) | 1 | 13/16 x 2 x 48 1/2 |
| Arched rails at top of frame (G) | 2 | 13/16 x 8 1/2 x 33 3/4 |
| Triangular-shaped panels (H) | 1 | 3/4 x 12 1/2 x 12 1/2 (makes both) |
| Blocks under pilasters (I) | 2 | 1 x 4 x 3 |
| Upper shelves (J) | 2 | 13/16 x 27 1/2 x 57 |
| Shelf and bottom (K) | 2 | 13/16 x 27 1/2 x 57 |
| Table shelf (L) | 1 | 13/16 x 28 5/16 x 57 |
| Stile between doors (M) | 1 | 13/16 x 4 x 29 1/2 |
| Stiles on doors (N) | 4 | 13/16 x 2 3/4 x 27 1/4 |
| Upper rails in doors (O) | 2 | 13/16 x 2 3/4 x 18 3/4 |
| Lower rails in doors (P) | 2 | 13/16 x 3 1/2 x 18 3/4 |
| Door panels (Q) | 2 | 3/4 x 15 1/2 x 21 3/4 |
| Crown molding (R) | | 2 3/4 x 72 (length needed to cut properly) |
| Molding above doors on table shelf (S) | 1 | 5/8 x 13/16 x 44 1/2 |
| Knotty-pine plywood backs (T) | 2 | 3/8 x 37 1/2 x 90 1/2 |
| H-L wrought-iron hinges (U) | 2 pair 3 in. | |
| Wrought iron latches (V) | 2 | |
| Quarter-round molding (W) | 1 | 1/2 x 45 1/4 |

tise them, and then make and fit the rails. Raise the panels in the same manner as the triangular-shaped ones. It should be noted that panels are never glued to the frames, but should be left loose in the grooves to which they are fitted. The reason is that with furnace heat in the house, they will shrink, and with the heat turned off in the summer, they will expand. When left unglued they will shrink and expand without splitting or buckling, provided they are properly fitted. Panels of this width should be made about ⅛ in. narrower than the place provided for them. The length need not be reduced since the wood will neither shrink nor swell appreciably in this direction.

Once the doors have been made, they should be carefully fitted to the openings. Since pine tends to shrink and expand considerably during changes of season even when the wood is well seasoned, the doors should be fitted accordingly. If the work is done during the summertime, when the wood normally has expanded as much as it will during any season of the year, the doors should be made to fit the openings rather closely. Some judgment in this matter must be used.

All that now remains to be done is to fit and fasten the cupboard into the corner where it belongs, to put the hinges and latches on the doors, and to apply whatever finish has been decided upon. Since the natural finish the writer gave this piece is the same as that applied to the trestle table, directions for doing it here will not be repeated.

# 3. Trestle Table of Knotty Pine

Fig. 16

The trestle table shown in Figure 16 is ideally suited for use in a library or living room, or as a dining table. While it is shown here set up as a dining table, it is normally used in the author's home as a library table back of a sofa.

The ease of construction is in no way commensurate with the great amount of service this piece of furniture renders. It is an ideal worktable. One may be seated comfortably at either side of the table, there being little or no interference from the table's supporting members. Its generous surface area is another feature to recommend it. The author built this table in a single day's working time.

To build the table, first glue up the top. While the glue is drying, cut the pieces for the feet, posts, cleats, and rail. Plane and square these to size. Shape the feet and cleats on the band saw. Lay out and cut the mortises in the posts, feet, and cleats. Cut and fit the tenons on the posts and rail. Lay out and cut all chamfers as shown in the drawing.

Drill slotted holes into the cleats to screw fast the top. They are made in this manner to prevent splitting of the top during different seasons of the year, caused by contraction or expansion of the wood.

Glue up the leg assemblies, consisting of the posts, cleats, and feet. Bore holes and drive pegs

into the joints, as shown in Figure 19.

Make a trial assembly of both legs and the rail, and at this point lay out the wedge-shaped mortises for the keys. Take out the rail and cut these mortises. Make the keys; then glue the rail to the posts, and drive in the keys to pull the joints tightly together. This will be possible if the wedge-shaped mortise is cut to within $1^{11}\!/_{16}$ in. of the shoulder on the rail.

Plane and sandpaper the top. Fasten the cleats to the top with wood screws. If the slotted holes are cut wide enough, washers may be used under the screwheads.

The author used a natural finish consisting of two coats of floor sealer, a hard durable finish which penetrates deeply into the wood. This was followed with two coats of satin-finish varnish. Each coat of finish was steel-wooled with #0 steel wool before the next coat was applied, and the final coat was steel-wooled, then waxed and polished.

## BILL OF MATERIAL

| DESCRIPTION | PIECES | DIMENSIONS |
| --- | --- | --- |
| Feet | 2 | 1¾ x 3 x 36 |
| Cleats under top | 2 | 1¾ x 3 x 36 |
| Posts | 2 | 1¾ x 5 x 28¼ |
| Rail | 1 | 2½ x 3 x 54¾ |
| Keys | 2 | ½ x 1½ x 4 |
| Top (when glued) | 1 | ¾ x 40 x 72 |

20

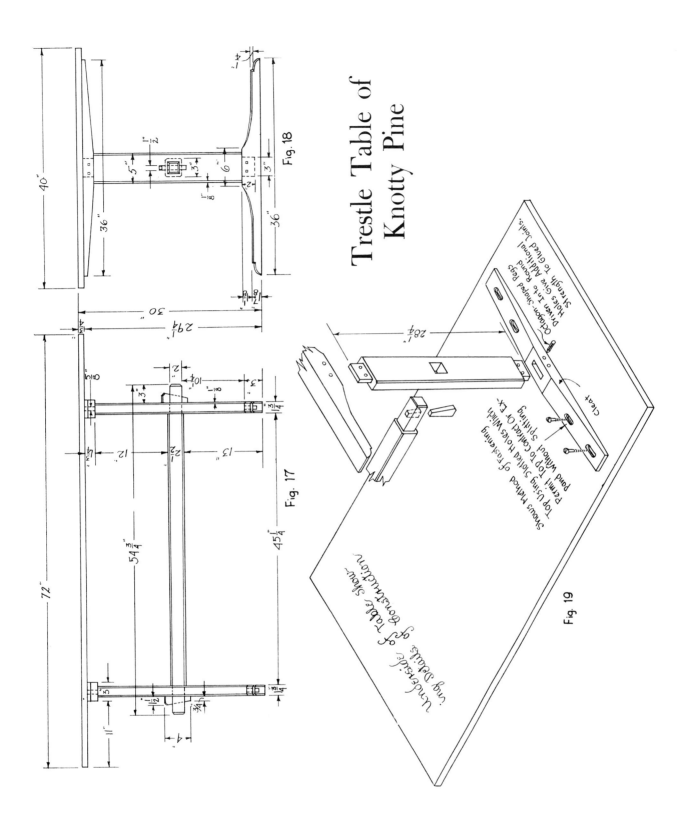

Trestle Table of Knotty Pine

Fig. 18

Fig. 17

Fig. 19

Underside of Table Showing Details of Construction.

Shows Method of Fastening
Top Using Slotted Holes Which
Permit Top to Contract Or Ex-
pand Without Splitting

Octagon-Shaped Peg
Driven Into Round
Holes Give Additional
Strength To Glued Joints.

Cleat

21

# 4. Occasional Table to Use in Front of a Sofa

Fig. 20

This interesting table (Fig. 20), intended to be placed in front of a sofa, will hold magazines, a lamp, and other items usually desired near a sofa. The drawers may hold playing cards, pencils, pen, and many other things. It may also be used as an end table by a sofa or easy chair, since its height and length are just about the same as those of a sofa arm. Its unique design and the dovetail-joint construction will make it a conversation piece in anybody's living room.

Because maple is a better wood for turning than pine, and also because it is much stronger and harder, the legs and stretchers should be made of this material. Maple and white pine used together need not be inharmonious.

To build the table, first turn the legs and stretchers. Also cut the rear stretcher, which is not

turned. If you do not have a board wide enough for the top into which the legs are to be fitted, glue one up to the proper width.

Boring the holes for slanting legs such as these is always something of a problem for the amateur woodworker. If it is to be done with hand tools, it is best to make a boring jig. This may consist of a fairly thick block of wood — let us say one about 1¾ by 6 by 6 in. Bore a hole in the middle of one side, and perpendicular to it. Then plane the lower side of the block to an angle which will coincide with that at which the leg holes are to be bored (Fig. 28). Clamp the block fast to the underside of the tabletop in the proper position to act as a guide for the bit while boring the holes.

If a drill press is available on which the table holding the work can be tilted both forward and to

22

# Occasional Table to Use
## in Front of a Sofa

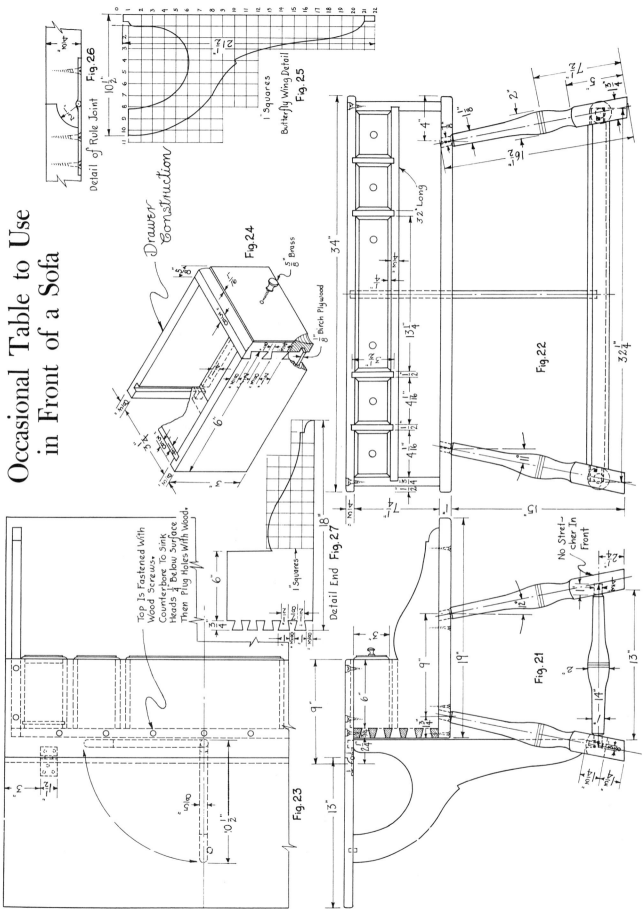

Detail of Rule Joint    Fig. 26

Butterfly Wing Detail    Fig. 25

1" Squares

Drawer Construction    Fig. 24

⅝" Brass

⅛" Birch Plywood

Fig. 22

34"

32¼"

32" Long

13¼"

Top Is Fastened With Wood Screws. Counterbore To Sink Heads ¼" Below Surface Then Plug Holes With Wood.

Fig. 23

10½"

9"

6"

Detail End    Fig. 27

18"

1" Squares

13"

9"

6"

No Stretcher In Front

Fig. 21

13"

19"

15"

7¼"

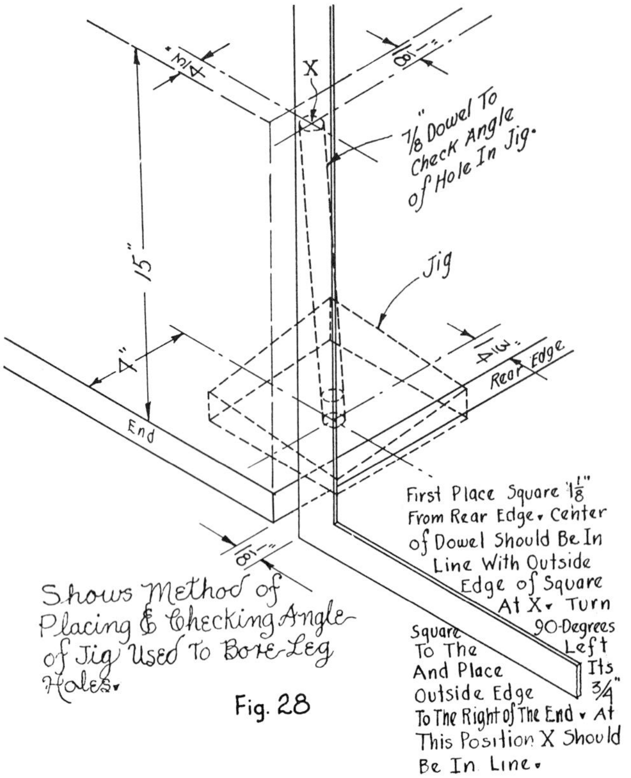
X
7/8" Dowel To Check Angle of Hole In Jig.
Jig
15"
4"
End
Rear Edge
First Place Square 1 1/8" From Rear Edge. Center of Dowel Should Be In Line With Outside Edge of Square At X. Turn Square 90-Degrees To The Left And Place Its Outside Edge 3/4" To The Right of The End. At This Position X Should Be In Line.

Shows Method of Placing & Checking Angle of Jig Used To Bore Leg Holes.

Fig. 28

either side, the boring angle may be easily obtained by tilting the table sideways to the angle shown in Figure 22, and forward to the angle shown in Figure 21. If the drill-press table tilts only sideways, a jig made of a block of wood which is placed under the work to tilt it forward to the proper angle will serve the purpose.

If a drill press is used to bore these holes, the author suggests using a board 12½ in. wide, drilling the holes which would then be the same distance from every corner, and afterward gluing on the additional 6½ in. to bring the top to its full 19-in. width.

Holes and mortises must now be cut into the bottoms of the legs so the stretchers may be joined to them. Once more, by properly tilting the legs, these may be made on a drill press or a mortising machine. If these machines are not available, the job may be done with hand tools, provided the angles are properly laid out. Laying out correct angles on the sides of the legs for boring or mortising will be easy once the legs have been put into the holes in the top, since lines parallel to the floor, at the proper height from the floor, will give these angles.

Glue the legs and stretchers together; then glue the legs into the holes which have been bored in the top, first making a saw kerf on the end of each leg and driving wedges into these, as shown in Figure 22. The glued-in wedges will lock the legs securely in place.

Next make the ends, back, the board which goes under the drawers, and the drawer partitions. Lay out and cut the grooves to join these together. Now make the part of the tabletop which goes over the drawers. Lay out and cut the grooves on this also, remembering that these grooves do not go all the way across the board (Fig. 21).

It is best to cut the grooves in the ends before cutting the dovetails. The dovetails on the ends and back may be laid out from the pattern of the end (Fig. 27). These may be cut on the band saw, once the lines have been accurately drawn. The pin members on the back may be cut on the circular saw, if it is placed vertically against the crosscutting fence, and if the crosscutting fence is set at the proper angle. Both may, of course, be cut out by hand with a dovetail saw and very sharp chisels.

Since the hinged leaf has a rule joint (Fig. 26), this should be made and properly hinged before assembling the upper part of the table. Also bore the hole under the top which holds the upper part of the butterfly wing. After the rule joint and

**BILL OF MATERIAL**

| DESCRIPTION | PIECES | DIMENSIONS |
|---|---|---|
| **Hard Rock Maple** | | |
| Legs | 4 | 2 x 2 x 16½ |
| Rear stretcher | 1 | 1¾ x 1¾ x 32¼ |
| Turned stretchers | 2 | 2-in. diam. x 14 in. |
| **Knotty Pine** | | |
| Top | 1 | 1 x 19 x 34 |
| Ends | 2 | ¾ x 7¼ x 18 |
| Back | 1 | ¾ x 7¼ x 33 |
| Board under drawers | 1 | ¾ x 6 x 32 |
| Tabletop | 1 | ¾ x 9 x 34 |
| Table leaf | 1 | ¾ x 13 x 34 |
| Butterfly wing | 1 | ⅝ x 10½ x 21½ |
| Partitions between drawers | 4 | ½ x 6 x 3½ |
| Drawer front | 1 | ⅝ x 3 x 13¼ |
| Drawer fronts | 4 | ⅝ x 3 x 4¹⁄₁₆ |
| **Clear Pine** | | |
| Drawer sides | 10 | ⅜ x 3 x 6 |
| Drawer back | 1 | ¼ x 2⅝ x 12⅞ |
| Drawer backs | 4 | ¼ x 2⅝ x 3⅝ |
| **Birch Plywood** | | |
| Drawer bottom | 1 | ⅛ x 12⅞ x 5⅞ |
| Drawer bottoms | 4 | ⅛ x 3⅝ x 5⅞ |
| Table-leaf hinges | 2 | |
| Brass knob drawer pulls | 6 | |

hinges have been properly fitted, remove the hinges in order to make it easier to assemble the parts comprising the upper part of the table.

Assemble the upper part first, gluing together the ends, back, and the board which goes under the drawers. When the glue has dried on these, remove the clamps and clean and dress all joints.

Next, glue fast the drawer partitions and the narrow part of the top above the drawers. Counterbore and drill the holes; then glue and screw fast this top and the partitions.

Locate and drill the holes through the wide top, to which the legs are fastened; for the insertion of wood screws to secure the upper part. Countersink these holes for the heads of the screws. Fasten this assembled upper section to the lower section, remembering that the butterfly wing must be put into place at this time. Then replace the hinges.

Working from the detail drawing (Fig. 24), make the drawers. A simpler rabbet and butt joint could be substituted for the dovetailed joint with which the drawer sides and fronts are joined together, but dovetailed joints are so much stronger and more attractive when they are made with the patience and skill they demand. A clearance of about 1/16 in. is enough for so small a drawer.

The choice of finish is optional, but if knotty pine is used as shown, the knots should not be obscured by an opaque finish, since they add so much to the beauty of the design.

# 5. Paneled Wastebasket

Fig. 29

The knotty-pine-paneled wastebasket (Fig. 29) is a distinctive and very useful small piece of furniture. While its slanting sides may present a stiff challenge to the amateur woodworker the result should be highly worth his effort. The warm beauty of the white pine, colored with a very transparent stain made from mixing burnt umber with turpentine, makes this piece attractive enough to be used with almost any other furniture. The raised panels, which are a part of this design, add greatly to its charm.

The parts comprising each of the basket's four sides are made first and then assembled. Plane and sandpaper all stock carefully. Cut the mortises on the stiles. If a drill press or mortising machine is available, a simple jig, like the one shown in Figure 33 may readily be used to do this part of the work.

The ends of the tenons on the rails are left square, while the shoulders must be slanted at a 12½-deg. angle, which may be set up on the sliding T bevel directly from Figure 30, or from a protractor.

Make the panels next, cutting them to the proper shape and size. In the sketch (Fig. 34) we show a good method for raising this and similar panels which are used on various projects throughout this book. The shallow grooves parallel to each edge, shown on the side of the panel in Figure 34, may be cut first, or these cuts may be made to take off the waste after performing the operation shown in Figure 34. This operation is performed by tilting either the saw table or the saw blade to an angle of 16 deg. The angle at which the saw needs to be tilted in raising panels of this kind is determined by the thickness of the panel and the width of the border desired around the panel. The operation is not a difficult one, once the saw setup has been properly made.

These sawed surfaces must then be smoothed with a scraper and sandpaper.

Do not glue the panels into the grooves. They should be loose in the frames. Glue only the mortise-and-tenon joints, and then drill ¼-in. holes through each one for the square pegs which are trimmed to a rough octagon shape before being driven into the round holes.

The angles at the bottoms of the frames may be

26

# Paneled Wastebasket

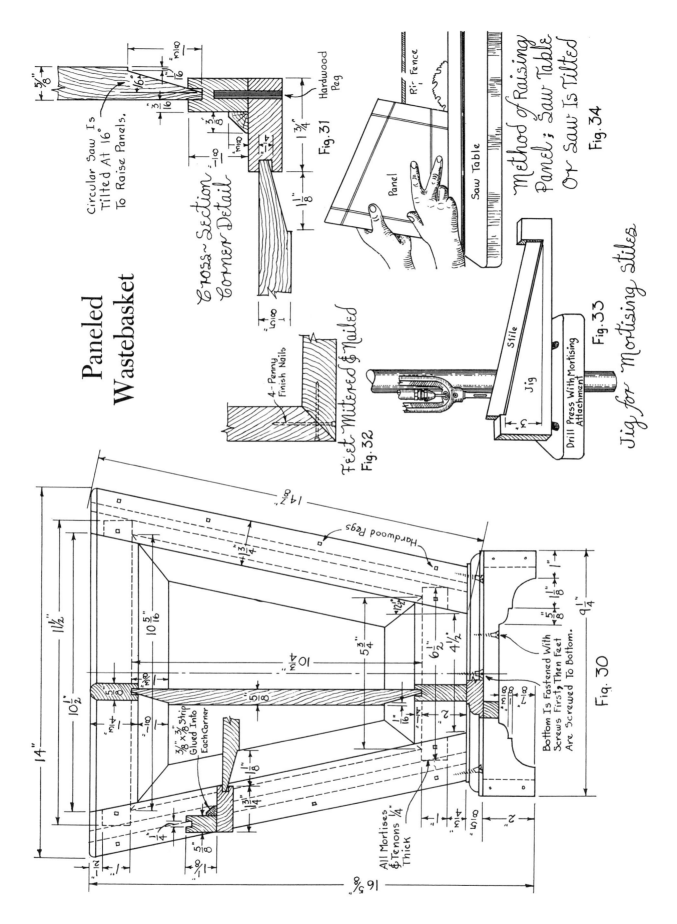

Circular Saw I's Tilted At 16° To Raise Panels.

Cross~Section Corner Detail

Fig. 31

Hardwood Peg

4-Penny Finish Nails

Feet Mitered & Nailed

Fig. 32

Ri Fence

Panel

Saw Table

Method of Raising Panel; Saw Table Or Saw Is Tilted

Fig. 34

Stile

Jig

Drill Press With Mortising Attachment

Jig for Mortising Stiles

Fig. 33

Hardwood Pegs

3/8" x 3/8" Strip Glued Into Each Corner

All Mortises & Tenons 1/4" Thick

Bottom Is Fastened With Screws First, Then Feet Are Screwed To Bottom.

Fig. 30

determined from Figure 30, or with a sliding T bevel. Plane the frames to fit squarely on the floor. Round the tops of the frames either before or after putting together the four sides of the wastebasket. Some of this rounding at the corners is easier after the sides have been pegged and glued together. Corner reinforcing strips, like those shown in Figure 31, make these joints more durable.

Mold the edges of the bottom to the shape indicated on either a regular shaper or with a portable hand shaper.

When the bottom has been made and fastened to the frames with wood screws, cut out and assemble the feet. These are also fastened with wood screws to the bottom. The corners of the feet are joined with miter joints, as shown in Figure 32.

After staining the wastebasket as we have sug-

## BILL OF MATERIAL

| DESCRIPTION | PIECES | DIMENSIONS |
| --- | --- | --- |
| Stiles | 4 | ⅝ x 1¾ x 14⅞ |
| Stiles | 4 | ⅝ x 1⅛ x 14⅞ |
| Upper rails | 4 | ⅝ x 1¾ x 11½ |
| Lower rails | 4 | ⅝ x 2 x 6½ |
| Panels | 4 | ⅝ x 10⁵⁄₁₆ x 10¾ |
| Bottom | 1 | ⅝ x 9¼ x 9¼ |
| Feet | 4 | ⅝ x 2 x 9¼ |
| Corner strips | 4 | ⅜ x ⅜ x 14⅜ |
| Hardwood pegs | | ¼ x ¼ x 1½ |

gested, give it a sealing coat of thin shellac, or some other good sealer. After it is thoroughly dry steel-wool the surface lightly to smooth it, and then apply several coats of varnish or other good finish. Rub down the final coat with pumice stone, apply a coat of floor wax, and polish.

Fig. 35

Knotty pine has, it seems, a peculiarly American flavor. It has a heartwarming quality, for one thing, which no other wood possesses. We think the folding screen, shown in Figure 35, reflects this quality. Furthermore, the white pine, which is used for the frames, is comparatively light in weight, making it ideal for this particular piece of furniture, which needs frequent moving about from place to place.

Plane and sandpaper all pieces smooth. Knotty pine, such as is used for the panels, should not be planed, but should be smoothed with a power sander, or scraped and then hand-sanded. Panels as wide as these must usually be glued up, though often it is possible to get boards wide enough. Note that the grain on all of these panels runs vertically, even that on the narrow panels in the middle.

# Folding Screen

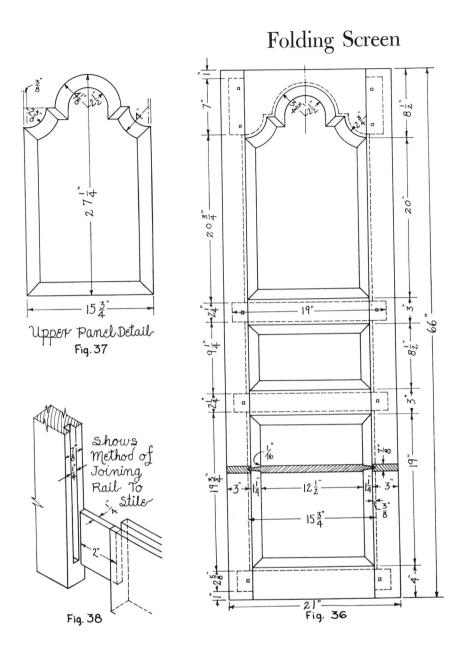

Upper Panel Detail
Fig. 37

Shows Method of Joining Rail To Stile

Fig. 38

Fig. 36

These panels may be raised in the same manner as those on the wastebasket in Project 5, where the process of panel raising is described in detail. On this project, however, it will be noticed that the panels must be raised on both sides, since both sides of the screen are equally important. Ten degrees is the angle at which the saw or saw table is tilted to raise these panels.

The tops of the upper panels, cannot, of course, be raised in the same manner as the other sides. Some of this work might be done on a shaper with proper cutters, but knives long enough to raise panels like these would hardly be safe to use on even a big heavy-duty shaper, so these parts are best carved by hand with wood-carving chisels. First, the outline of the inside curves is made with a V tool, then the shaping is finished with extra flats and a skew chisel. The operation should not prove difficult.

Once the joints have all been made, and the panels properly fitted, the frames may be glued up. All mortise-and-tenon joints are pegged, as well as glued together. No glue is put on the panels, or in the grooves into which they fit. These should be snug, but not tight in the frames, and not quite as wide as the space provided for them.

Special double-acting hinges are available for building folding screens, and these should be used to join the three parts of the screen together, as shown in Figure 35. Such hinges permit the screen to be folded or opened in either a forward or backward direction.

## BILL OF MATERIAL

| DESCRIPTION | PIECES | DIMENSION |
|---|---|---|
| Stiles | 6 | ⅞ x 3 x 66 |
| Top rails | 3 | ⅞ x 8½ x 19 |
| Middle rails | 6 | ⅞ x 3 x 19 |
| Bottom rails | 3 | ⅞ x 4 x 19 |
| Upper panels | 3 | ⅞ x 15¾ x 27¼ |
| Middle panels | 3 | ⅞ x 15¾ x 9¼ |
| Lower panels | 3 | ⅞ x 15¾ x 19¾ |
| Double-acting folding screen hinges, brass plated | 6 | 1¾ x 1⅛ |

# 7. Spice Cabinets

Fig. 39

While spice cabinets is the name given to them, the term hardly encompasses the varied uses to which these attractive little nests of drawers may be put. Cabinets like these often were used to hold spices in the kitchens of early American homes, but many other uses will suggest themselves to the person wishing to make them. The carved sunburst at the top of both is an engaging bit of decoration.

White pine, with a natural satin finish was used. The small brass drawer pulls add a distinctive touch to the general appearance.

Cut out the back and ends first. The sunburst should be carved after the back has been cut to

## BILL OF MATERIAL

| DESCRIPTION | PIECES | DIMENSIONS |
| --- | --- | --- |
| **Four-Drawer Cabinet** | | |
| Ends | 2 | ½ x 5 x 16½ |
| Back | 1 | ½ x 4¼ x 19 |
| Bottom | 1 | ½ x 5½ x 5¾ |
| Shelves | 4 | ½ x 4½ x 4¼ |
| Drawer fronts | 3 | ½ x 3¼ x 4 |
| Drawer front | 1 | ½ x 3⅛ x 4 |
| Drawer sides | 8 | ¼ x 2¹⁵⁄₁₆ x 4½ |
| Drawer bottoms (plywood) | 4 | ⅛ x 3⁷⁄₁₆ x 4⅜ |
| Drawer backs | 4 | ¼ x 2⁷⁄₁₆ x 3⁷⁄₁₆ |
| **Seven-Drawer Cabinet** | | |
| Ends | 2 | ½ x 5 x 16½ |
| Back | 1 | ½ x 8½ x 19 |
| Bottom | 1 | ½ x 5½ x 10 |
| Shelves | 4 | ½ x 4½ x 8½ |
| Partitions | 3 | ½ x 4½ x 3⅛ |
| Drawer fronts | 6 | ½ x 3¼ x 4 |
| Drawer front | 1 | ½ x 3⅛ x 8¼ |
| Drawer sides | 8 | ¼ x 2¹⁵⁄₁₆ x 4½ |
| Drawer bottoms (plywood) | 6 | ⅛ x 3⁷⁄₁₆ x 4⅜ |
| Drawer bottom | 1 | ⅛ x 4⅜ x 7⁷⁄₁₆ |
| Drawer backs | 6 | ¼ x 2⁷⁄₁₆ x 3⁷⁄₁₆ |
| Drawer back | 1 | ¼ x 2⁷⁄₁₆ x 7¹¹⁄₁₆ |

size and sandpapered. The ends should then be grooved for the shelves, and rabbeted at the rear edges for the back.

Assemble the ends, shelves, and back. Then cut molding around three edges of the bottom with a shaper, and fasten the bottom to the back and sides with wood screws.

Drawers are made last. The fronts are made and sanded smooth. Make and join together all parts for the drawers, leaving about ¹⁄₁₆-in. clearance for the drawer to fit the opening properly. When all drawers have been fitted, give the job a good finish.

The ones shown in Figure 39 were finished to preserve the natural color of the wood as much as possible. Two others which the author built at the same time were given a transparent coat of stain, made by tinting turpentine with a small amount of burnt umber; just enough to let the grain show through clearly when the stain had been wiped off. A sealer coat of thinned shellac, followed by several coats of varnish, or lacquer, with the final coat rubbed down with pumice stone and oil to a smooth gloss is recommended.

In the past several years, a number of very good, quick drying finishing materials which dry dust-free in a matter of minutes have come on the market. Some of these hardly change the color of the wood at all, so they are excellent where the natural beauty of the wood should be preserved, or even enhanced. New water stains which do not raise wood grain are also available. Such finishes are well worth trying on projects in this book where the natural beauty of the grain is to be preserved.

Putting on the brass drawer pulls completes the making of the spice cabinets.

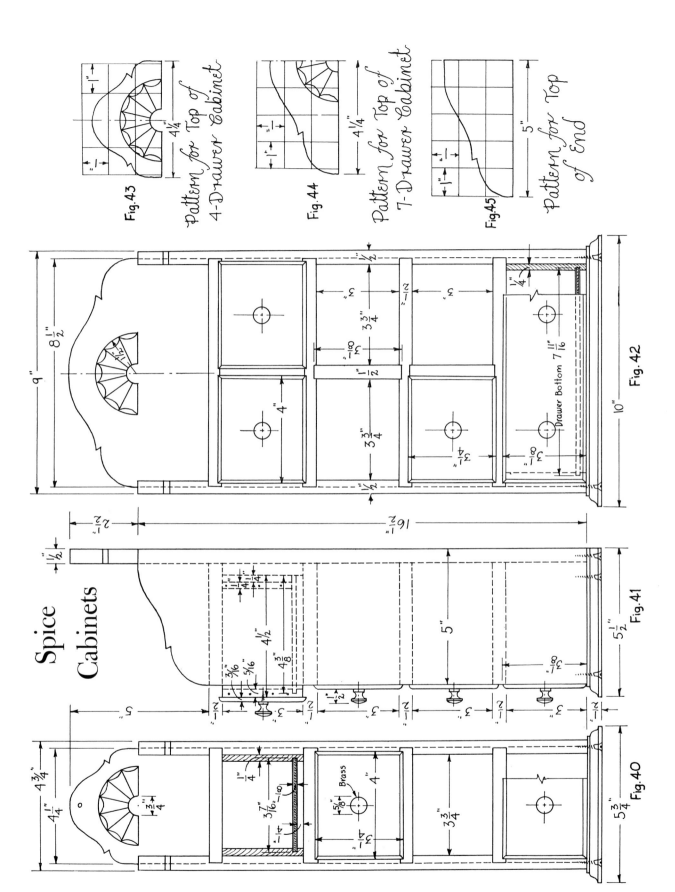

Spice Cabinets

Fig. 43

Pattern for Top of 4-Drawer Cabinet

Fig. 44

Pattern for Top of 7-Drawer Cabinet

Fig. 45

Pattern for Top of End

Fig. 40

Fig. 41

Fig. 42

33

# 8.  Wall Cabinet for China or Condiments

Fig. 46

The little wall cabinet, shown in Figure 46, was designed to hold a tea set, to be used when entertaining a few guests. It is ideal for the purpose, being just large enough to hold the few pieces of china required. Besides serving a useful function, it constitutes a very welcome and interesting addition to the other dining room furniture, adding a note of hospitality. Used in the kitchen, this cabinet could serve to hold spices and condiments.

The design has purposely been kept simple in accord with the function it is to serve. This makes it a suitable project for the home or school shop. Even the doors, which on a project like this are often the most difficult members to build, are easily within the scope of the equipment and ability

range usually found in school or even home workshops (Fig. 49).

The cabinet proper is little more than a box nailed together with finishing nails. It may be made of white pine or poplar.

The pediment effect is achieved by a face board nailed to both ends at the top (Figs. 47 and 48). This face board is formed with a break in its center, and appropriately ornamented with molding, dentils, and a classic urn finial. Little difficulty should be encountered in building the pediment, except in the fitting of the short return moldings in the break and at the ends of the board.

The short pieces in the break of the pediment will be wider than the molding on the face of the

34

# Wall Cabinet for China or Condiments

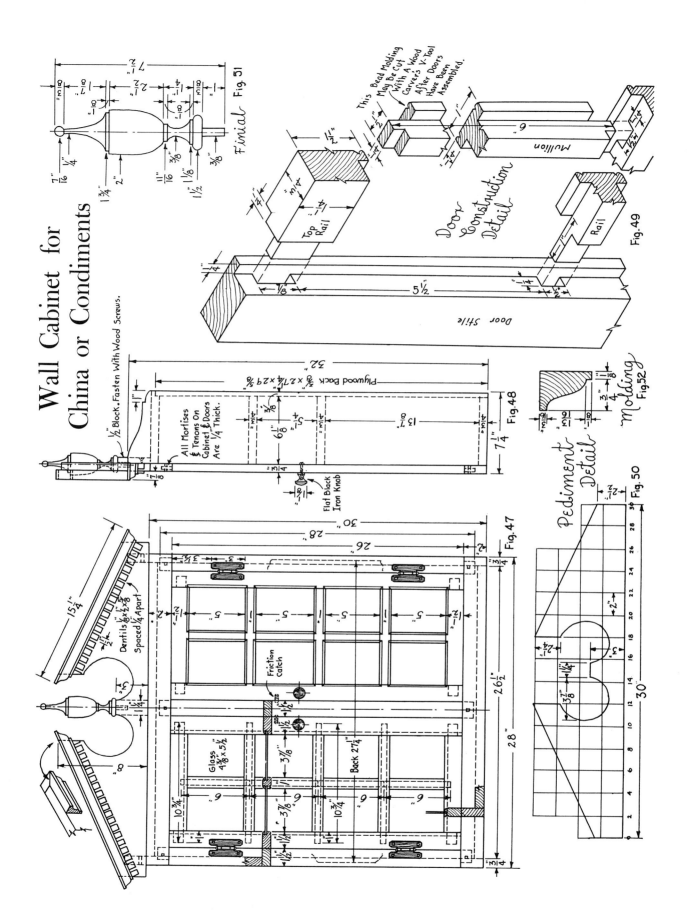

Finial Fig. 51

This Bead Molding May Be Cut With A Wood Carver's V-Tool After Doors Have Been Assembled.

Door Construction Detail

Mullion

Top Rail

Rail

Fig. 49

Door Stile

½" Block. Fasten With Wood Screws.

All Mortises & Tenons On Cabinet & Doors Are ¼" Thick.

Plywood Back ⅜" x 27¼ x 24⅝

Fig. 48

Flat Black Iron Knob

Molding Fig. 52

Pediment Detail

Fig. 50

Dentils ⅛" x 2 x ⅜ Spaced ¼" Apart

Friction Catch

Glass 4⅞ x 5½

Back 27¼

Fig. 47

board, while the pieces at the ends will be narrower. When the cabinet shown in Figure 46 was built, plain blocks of wood were glued and bradded to these places, and then hand-carved to the proper shape.

The miters at the corners are what are commonly known as compound miters; that is, the face molding must be held at the angle at which it is fastened to the board when the miter cut is being made to properly join it to the return molding. Fitting these moldings to each other accurately will constitute an important lesson in advanced cabinet-making.

When completed, the cabinet was given an undercoat of paint, followed by two coats of light ivory enamel. The black H hinges greatly enhance the appearance of a cabinet such as this.

## BILL OF MATERIAL

| DESCRIPTION | PIECES | DIMENSIONS |
| --- | --- | --- |
| Ends | 2 | ¾ x 6½ x 32 |
| Pediment | 1 | ¾ x 8 x 30 |
| Top rail | 1 | ¾ x 2 x 28 |
| Bottom rail | 1 | ¾ x 2 x 28 |
| Stiles | 3 | ¾ x 1½ x 28 |
| Top | 1 | ¾ x 6½ x 26½ |
| Bottom | 1 | ¾ x 6⅛ x 26½ |
| Shelves | 2 | ¾ x 6⅛ x 26½ |
| Block under finial | | ½ x 1¼ x 3 |
| Finial | 1 | 2-in. diam. x 7½ |
| Door stiles | 4 | ¾ x 1½ x 26 |
| Door rails | 4 | ¾ x 1½ x 10¾ |
| Door rails | 6 | ¾ x 1 x 10¾ |
| Door mullions | 8 | ¾ x 1 x 6 |
| Flat-back H hinges | 4 | |
| Dentils, as needed | | ⅛ x ½ x ⅝ |
| Back (plywood) | 1 | ⅜ x 27¼ x 29⅝ |

# 9. Blanket Chest and Seat

Fig. 53

Blanket chests are especially useful in a bedroom; doubly so is one which may be used as a bench as well as a chest. The seat is provided with sides and a back so that a cushion made for it will not slide off when the lid is raised.

The chest features dovetail joints. Besides being one of the best ways to put a chest together, dovetail joints are a superb decorative feature.

Through dovetails like these may be cut on the band and circular saws, if care is used to work exactly to the layout lines. The tail members, on the front and back, may be cut on the band saw. The pin members, which are cut on the ends of the chest (Fig. 56), may be done on the circular saw, using the crosscutting fence set at an angle of 19 deg. The ends are placed in a vertical position against the crosscutting fence to make these cuts. It is best, perhaps, to make the pin members first, and then scribe lines for the tail members, using the end to be joined to it as a pattern. This should insure a perfect joint.

A molding, like the one shown, should be cut on the strip which is to be fastened to the lid, and to the upper edges of the members which make the feet. The feet are joined with a miter at the front. At the back they are nailed to a 2-in. strip, fitted between the two, and to the chest. The bottom of the chest is nailed fast to the inside of the chest before the feet are put on.

Enough detail is shown on the drawings in Figures 54 to 57 inclusive to make clear the remaining construction procedure.

In Figure 57 is shown the type of hinge and lid support recommended for the chest, because it is strong and durable, and because it pulls the top of the seat stretcher far enough forward to clear the wall when the lid is raised.

Poplar is the best wood to use in making this chest because its grain is firm enough to make good dovetail joints and because it is still possible to procure wide boards in this kind of lumber at a reasonable price.

## BILL OF MATERIAL

| DESCRIPTION | PIECES | DIMENSION |
|---|---|---|
| Front and back | 2 | ¾ x 15¼ x 46½ |
| Ends | 2 | ¾ x 15¼ x 20 |
| Bottom | 1 | ¾ x 18½ x 45 |
| Lid | 1 | ¾ x 20 x 46½ |
| Strip on front edge of lid | 1 | ¾ x 1¼ x 48 |
| Seat ends on lid | 2 | ¾ x 6 x 20¾ |
| Seat back on lid | 1 | ¾ x 4 x 48 |
| Feet at front | 1 | ¾ x 4 x 48 |
| Feet at ends | 2 | ¾ x 4 x 20¾ |
| Strip under chest, between feet at back | 1 | ¾ x 2 x 46½ |
| Chest hinges | 2 | |

# Blanket Chest & Seat With Dovetailed Corners

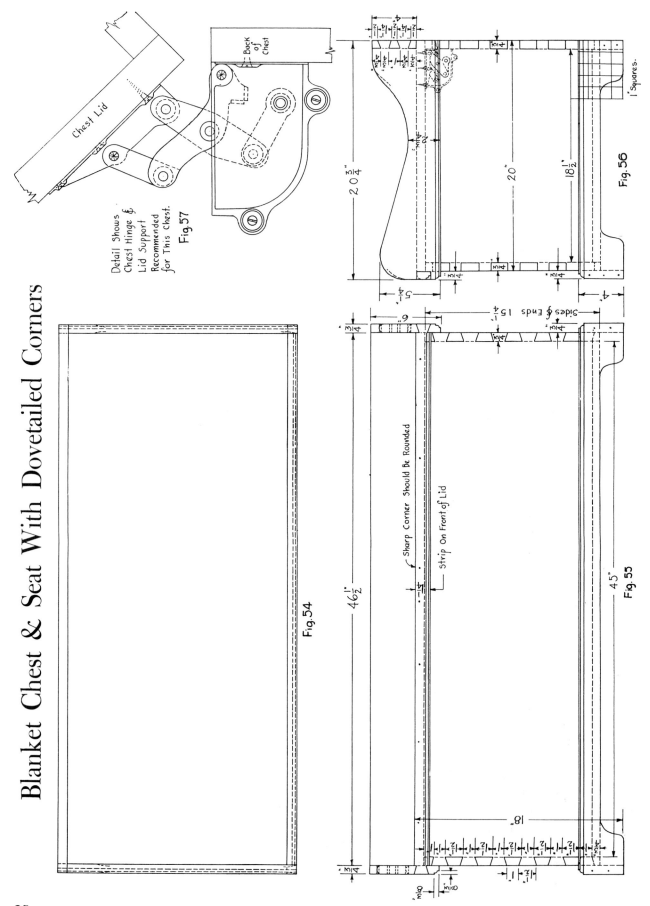

Chest Lid

Back of Chest

Detail Shows Chest Hinge & Lid Support Recommended for This Chest.
Fig. 57

Fig. 54

Fig. 56

Fig. 55

20 $\frac{3}{4}$"

20"

18 $\frac{1}{2}$"

1" Squares.

Sides & Ends 15 $\frac{1}{4}$"

6"

Sharp Corner Should Be Rounded

Strip On Front of Lid

46 $\frac{1}{2}$"

45"

18"

# 10. Drop-Leaf Table

Fig. 58

In rural areas of eastern Pennsylvania, where the author lives, drop-leaf tables like the one shown in Figure 58 are in great demand, both for the dining room and the kitchen. Many families own as many as three. While the better ones are made of cherry, many others are made of poplar or maple woods which, if given a good finish, are about as handsome as the more expensive material. The author owns a table on which the top is cherry, and the rest, even the turned legs, is poplar. One reason these tables are so well liked is that they give the sitter plenty of leg room, and also that, when not in use, with both leaves dropped, they take up so little floor space.

Usually, the legs on these tables are turned, but this one was designed as simple as possible so that it may be made in the workshop that does not have a lathe. In appearance it is almost as attractive as one with good turned legs: in fact, many people may prefer the plain tapered leg.

Tapering on these legs should start about 7 in. from the top, so all areas where joints have to be made will be wholly square. Since the swinging leg and apron need to come flush with the outside of the apron and leg against which it is swung when the leaves are dropped, the side aprons need to be made of several individual parts joined together as shown in Figures 59, 60, 61, and 62. Observe, for example, that the tenons are not made on both

ends of the same piece on the side aprons (Fig. 59). Furthermore, while the swinging leg, which is shown in Figure 59, swings to the right to close, the one on the opposite side, if it were shown, would be found to swing to the left to close, so that the table makes a better balanced appearance with both legs closed than if both swung toward the same end.

No great difficulty should be experienced in constructing the table. The making of a good finger joint (Fig. 63) may require special care, but if

## BILL OF MATERIAL

| DESCRIPTION | PIECES | DIMENSIONS |
|---|---|---|
| Legs | 6 | 1½ x 1½ x 28¼ |
| Aprons (F) | 2 | ¾ x 5 x 33¾ |
| Aprons (E) | 2 | ¾ x 5 x 17¾ |
| Blocks (G) | 2 | ¾ x 5 x 2¾ |
| Aprons on swinging legs (I) | 2 | ¾ x 5 x 13¼ |
| Stretchers above and below drawer | 2 | ¾ x 1½ x 19½ |
| Rear apron (H) | 1 | ¾ x 5 x 19½ |
| Middle part of top | 1 | ¾ x 22½ x 40 |
| Drop leaves | 2 | ¾ x 15 x 40 |
| Drawer front | 1 | ¾ x 3⁷⁄₁₆ x 17¹⁵⁄₁₆ |
| Drawer sides | 2 | ½ x 3⁷⁄₁₆ x 17¾ |
| Drawer runs | 2 | ¾ x ¾ x 16¼ |
| Strips to fasten top | 2 | ¾ x ¾ x 33 |
| Drawer bottom (plywood) | 1 | ¼ x 17⅜ x 17½ |
| Drawer back | 1 | ⅜ x 2¹³⁄₁₆ x 17⅜ |
| Dowel rods | 2 | ⁵⁄₁₆ x 4⅝ |
| Table-leaf hinges | 4 | 1¼ x 2⅞ |

39

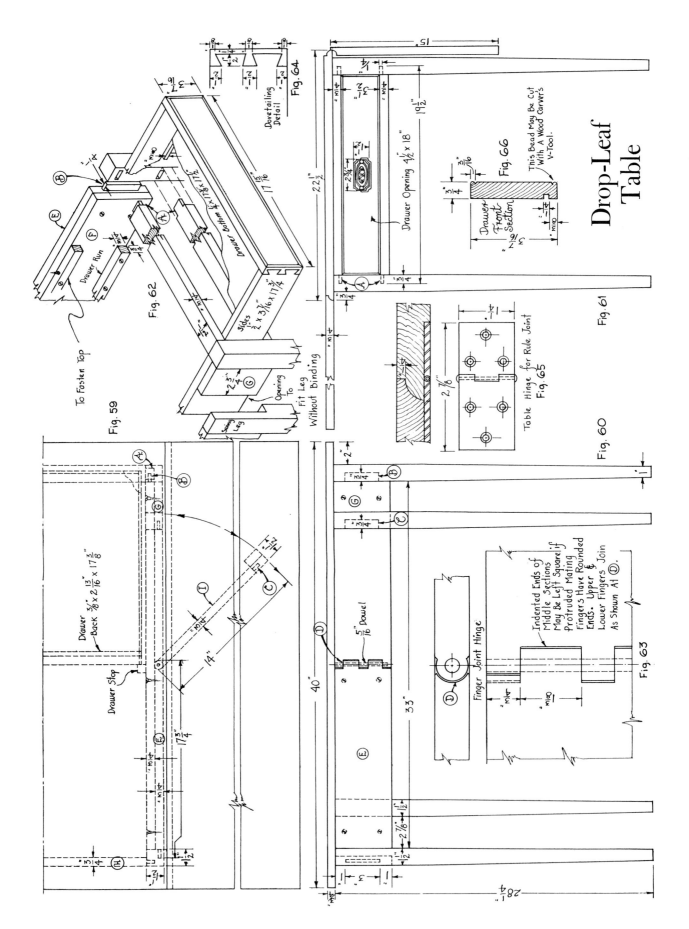

Drop-Leaf Table

Fig. 59
Fig. 60
Fig. 61
Fig. 62
Fig. 63
Fig. 64
Fig. 65
Fig. 66

40

made as directed, it should fit well, and should give good service. The question has often come up in making finger joints, why should the wooden dowel be used in making the hinges instead of a metal rod which would appear to be stronger. The reason, so far as the author has been able to ascertain, is that metal rods tend to rust or corrode and thus cause greater wear in the joint than the wooden one. Be that as it may, the author does not recollect ever having seen a metal one on an old table.

Rule joints are made to join the leaves to the central section, as shown in Figure 65. Figure 65 also shows the type of hinge which must be used to drop the leaves properly. These are always sunk flush with the underside of the leaves and middle section, and the barrel of the hinge should be centered in line with the straight section of the rule joint on the upper surface of the tabletop.

Although the blind dovetailed drawer joints are best and more attractive, a simpler drawer joint could readily be substituted.

# 11. Card Table With Revolving Top

Fig. 67

Many card tables, being but indifferent looking pieces of furniture are folded up after each use and tucked away in a closet until needed again. The possessor of this card table, however, will not want to hide it (Fig. 67). It is designed to serve a number of purposes; for example as a hall table under a dressing mirror or as a small serving table in the dining room. Its splayed legs give it a pert, as well as a smart, look. If made of maple, with, let us say, a beautifully grained top, it will be something to admire.

As the name suggests, the top is made to be revolved, so that when the short leaf, which is in a vertical position in Figure 70 is placed in a horizontal position, and the top turned 90 deg., it will lie on the legs as shown by the dotted lines, and will make a 34-in. square playing surface — very generous size for a card-table top.

Constructing the table presents no great difficulties. Working with oblique angles as you do here when joining stretchers to legs, is not as simple as joining the same parts at right angles. Mortises here are cut into the legs at an angle. Laying these angles out on the outside of each leg before the mortises are cut will help make this part of the work easier to accomplish. If the mortising is done on a drill press or on a mortising machine, the correct angles to tilt the work for doing it may be taken from Figures 72 and 73. It will be necessary to make the aprons slightly wider than the 4 in. shown in Figure 69 to allow for the angle to which their upper edges must be planed so they will come level with the tops of the legs. This extra width will be about ⅛ in. on the short aprons, and about

¹⁄₁₆ in. on the long ones, as indicated in our Bill of Material.

The top is revolved by fastening the wooden disk underneath the wide member, as shown in Figures 68 and 69. Figure 71 shows in greater detail the rotating mechanism and how it is used.

If so desired, Soss invisible hinges may be substituted for the card-table hinges shown here. If this is done, three hinges should be used. They would be mortised into the adjoining edges of the tops, and would not show when both leaves lie flat on the table.

## BILL OF MATERIAL

| DESCRIPTION | PIECES | DIMENSIONS |
|---|---|---|
| Legs | 4 | 1¾ x 1¾ x 27¾ |
| Aprons | 2 | ¾ x 4¹⁄₁₆ x 23½ |
| Aprons | 2 | ¾ x 4⅛ x 16⅞ |
| Top | 1 | ¹³⁄₁₆ x 21 x 34 |
| Top | 1 | ¹³⁄₁₆ x 13 x 34 |
| Glue blocks | 4 | ¾ x 2⅝ x 2 |
| Crosspiece | 1 | ¾ x 5 x 16⅝ |
| Disk | 1 | ¾ x 2¾-in. diam. |
| Machine bolt with washer and wing nut | 1 | ⅜ x 3 |
| Card-table hinges | 2 | |
| or | | |
| Soss invisible hinges | 3 | |

# Card Table With Revolving Top

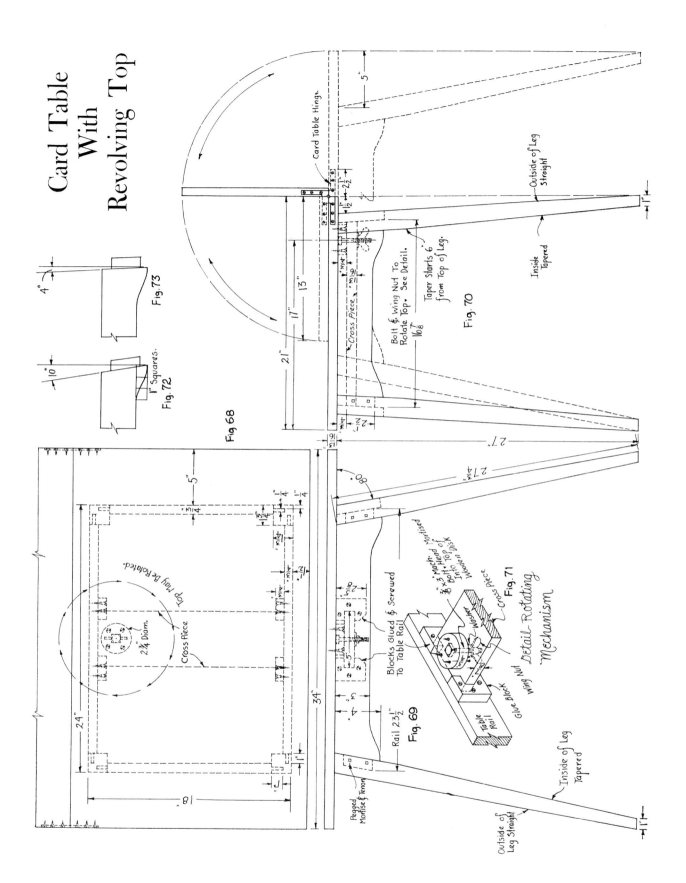

Fig. 73

Fig. 72

1" Squares.

Fig 68

Top May Be Rotated.

2¾" Diam.

Cross Piece

24"

5"

18

Card Table Hinge

21"

17"

13"

Cross Piece

Bolt & Wing Nut To
Rotate Top • See Detail.

16⅞"

Taper Starts 6"
from Top of Leg.

Fig. 70

Outside of Leg
Straight

Inside
Tapered

27"

27¼"

80°

Blocks Glued & Screwed
To Table Rail

Rail 23½"

Fig. 69

Pegged
Mortise & Tenon

Outside of
Leg Straight

Inside of Leg
Tapered

⅜" × 3" Mach.
Bolt • Top of
Bolt Head Mortised
Into Wooden Disk

Washer

Cross Piece

Wing Nut

Glue Block

Table Rail

Fig. 71 Detail Rotating
Mechanism

43

## 12. Bookshelves

Fig. 74

One seldom wishes to store books out of sight because, although a book's greatest value lies in what is to be found between its covers, the bindings and colorful jackets found on most books today do have real decorative value in a good furnishing scheme. A bookcase like the one shown in Figure 74 is therefore a most desirable addition to a room.

Few of the projects in this book are easier to construct than this one.

Dadoes are cut nearly all the way across the ends to join the shelves to them. These may be cut by hand with a router plane, with a portable electric hand router, or with a dado head on the circular saw. Since they are stopped dadoes, the ends will have to be finished with a hand chisel.

The top is nailed on with 6-penny finishing nails. Rabbeted edges are cut at the back of the top and ends for the plywood back, as shown in Figures 75 and 76.

Bracket feet are cut on the front of the base, but the ends are kept plain, except for the molding on the top edges. The corners are put together with miter joints.

### BILL OF MATERIAL

| DESCRIPTION | PIECES | DIMENSIONS |
|---|---|---|
| Ends | 2 | ¾ x 9 x 47¾ |
| Shelves | 4 | ¾ x 8¾ x 30½ |
| Front feet | 1 | ¾ x 4½ x 33 |
| End feet | 2 | ¾ x 4½ x 9¾ |
| Back (plywood) | 1 | ¼ x 30¾ x 44½ |

# Bookshelves

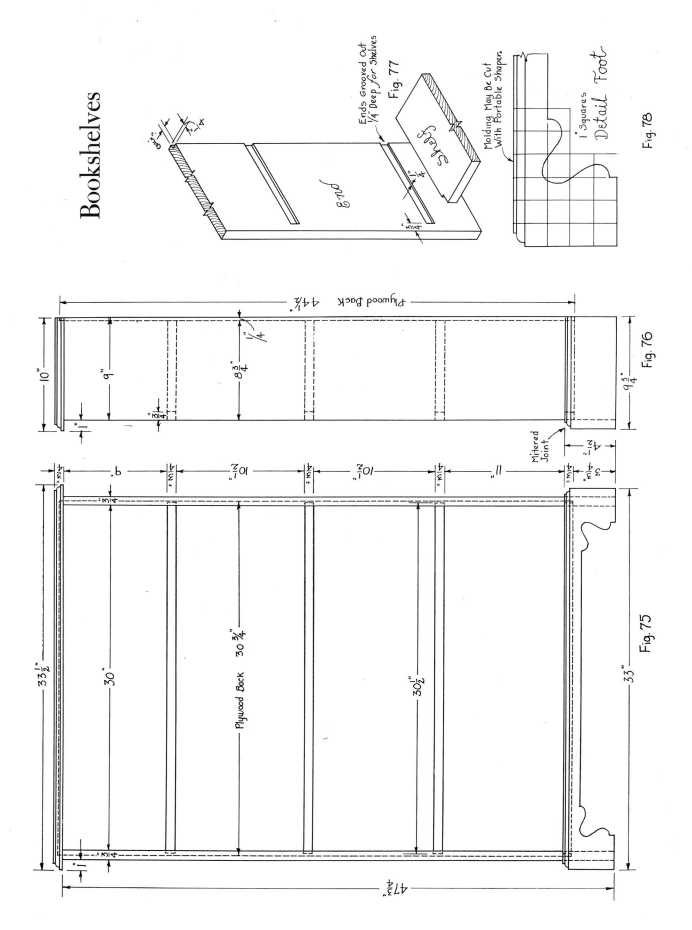

Ends Grooved Out
1/4 Deep for Shelves

Fig. 77

Shelf

End

Molding May Be Cut
With Portable Shaper.

1" Squares

Detail Foot

Fig. 78

Plywood Back 44½"

Mitered Joint

Fig. 76

Plywood Back 30¾"

Fig. 75

45

# 13. Cabinet With Sliding Doors

Fig. 79

The charm and usefulness of this small cabinet with the sliding doors can be seen in Figure 79. The upper shelves will hold books and small objects of decorative value, while the cupboard space behind the sliding doors provides needed storage space for many things.

The construction is quite simple. Shelf, floor, top, and track strip are nailed to the ends with finishing nails. The two tracks for the sliding doors are separated a distance of ⅛ in., or perhaps a little less, and are grooved into the bottom of the shelf, and into the track strip which is nailed to the front edge of the bottom. As indicated in Figure 83, the tracks should give sufficient clearance to the doors to insure easy sliding.

Back edges of the ends and top are rabbeted,

# Cabinet With Sliding Doors

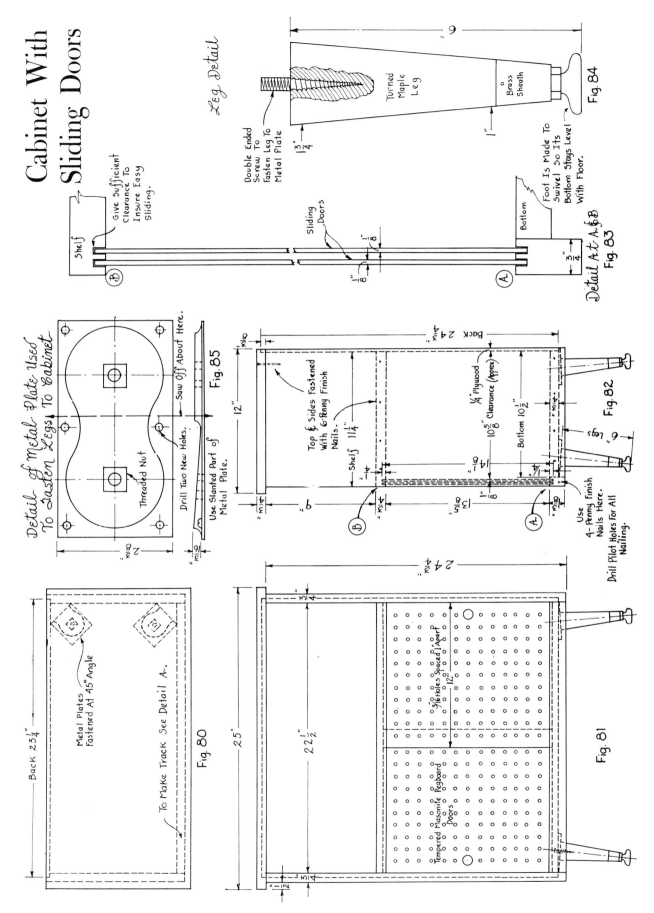

*Leg Detail*

Double Ended Screw To Fasten Leg To Metal Plate

Turned Maple Leg

Brass Sheath

Fig. 84

Give Sufficient Clearance To Insure Easy Sliding.

Shelf

Sliding Doors

Bottom

Foot Is Made To Swivel So Its Bottom Stays Level With Floor.

Detail At A & B
Fig. 83

Detail of Metal Plate Used To Fasten Legs To Cabinet

Threaded Nut

Drill Two New Holes.

Saw Off About Here.

Use Slanted Part of Metal Plate.

Fig. 85

Top & Sides Fastened With 6-Penny Finish Nails.

Shelf 11¼"

Back 24¼"

¼ Plywood

10⅝" Clearance (Approx)

Bottom 10½"

6" Legs

Use 4-Penny Finish Nails Here.

Drill Pilot Holes For All Nailing.

Fig. 82

Metal Plates Fastened At 45° Angle

To Make Track See Detail A.

Back 25¼"

Fig. 80

24¼"

22½"

25"

3/16 Holes Spaced 1" Apart

12"

Tempered Masonite Pegboard Doors

Fig. 81

47

so the back may be recessed, and nailed without any of its edges showing.

Legs of the kind shown may be bought cheaply, ready-made. They have nylon feet for easy sliding, and the brass sheath allows the foot to swivel so the bottom always sits level on the floor, even when the leg is slanted. A double-ended screw at the upper end of the leg is screwed fast to a metal plate, shown in Figure 85. Since the legs on this cabinet are to be slanted, the half of the plate which would hold the leg vertical is sawed off, as shown in Figure 85, so the rest of the plate may

be fastened close to the corner. The position of the plates is shown in Figure 80.

## BILL OF MATERIAL

| DESCRIPTION | PIECES | DIMENSIONS |
|---|---|---|
| Ends | 2 | ¾ x 11½ x 24¾ |
| Top | 1 | ¾ x 12 x 25 |
| Shelf | 1 | ¾ x 11¼ x 22½ |
| Bottom | 1 | ¾ x 10½ x 22½ |
| Track strip | 1 | ¾ x 1⅜ x 22½ |
| Back (plywood) | 1 | ¼ x 24¾ x 23¼ |
| Doors (tempered pegboard) | 2 | ⅛ x 12 x 14⅛ |
| Legs (maple) | 4 | 1¾ x 6 |

# 14.  Crèche for Christmas

A crèche at Christmastime reminds us, amid all the gay festivities, what Christmas really stands for. The simple little figurines in and around the miniature stable, shown in the lower shelf of the corner cupboard (Fig. 9 and in Fig. 88-A below), can be purchased in almost any 10-cent store. The stable may be made in a single evening of small bits of wood salvaged from the scrap pile found in almost any workshop.

The timbers of this one were made of white pine, cut ⅝ in. square on the circular saw, left unplaned, and then stained brown with burnt umber mixed with turpentine. The roof boards were scrap pieces of red cedar siding. The back and bottom were made of small pieces of plywood. Small brads were used to secure everything.

Placed at a point of vantage in the home, with the figurines set up with a different background each year, the crèche becomes an important focal point in the author's home during the Christmas season. He hopes it will do the same in the home of anyone who makes a reproduction of it.

## BILL OF MATERIAL

| DESCRIPTION | PIECES | DIMENSIONS |
| --- | --- | --- |
| Posts | 4 | ⅝ x ⅝ x 7 |
| Crossbeams | 2 | ⅝ x ⅝ x 14 |
| End beams | 2 | ⅝ x ⅝ x 5 |
| Rafters | 4 | ⅝ x ⅝ x 8⅛ |
| Rafter supports | 2 | ⅝ x ⅝ x 2 |
| Braces | 8 | ⅝ x ⅝ x 2½ |
| Red-cedar siding for roof | 2 | ¾ x 7 x 9¾ |
| Base (plywood) | 1 | ¼ x 6¼ x 14 |
| Back (plywood) | 1 | ¼ x 10½ x 14 |

Fig. 88-A

# Crèche

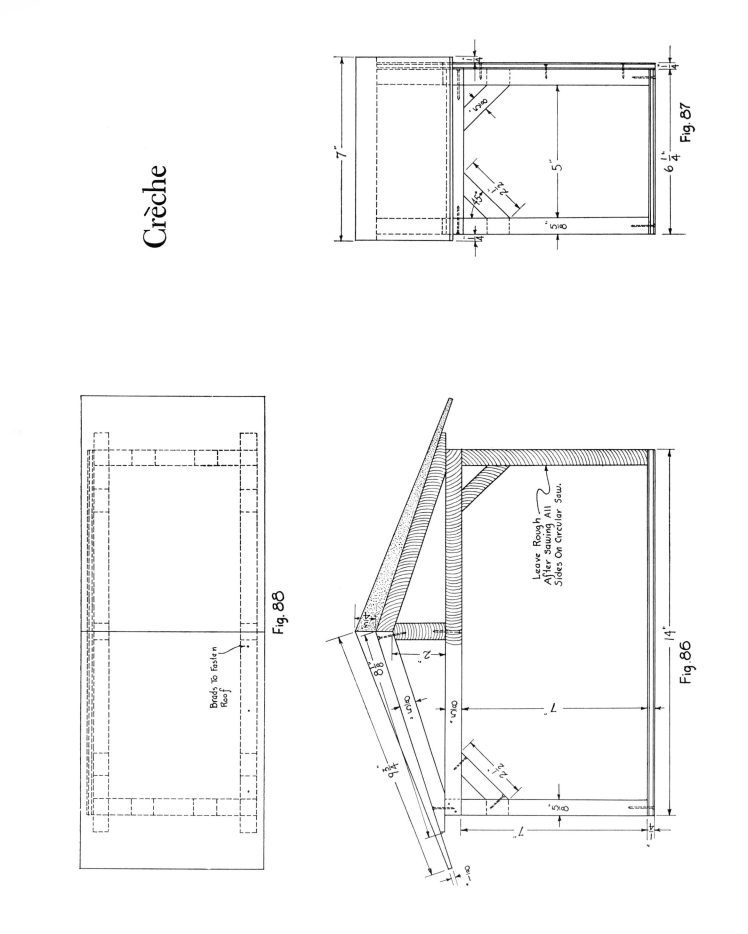

Fig. 87

Fig. 88

Brads To Fasten Roof

Leave Rough After Sawing All Sides On Circular Saw.

Fig. 86

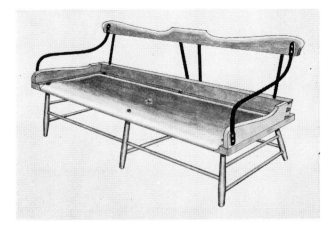

# 15. Settee

Fig. 89

The settee, shown in Figure 89, reminds one somewhat of an oldtime wagon seat. It is a bit different from the traditional type of settee so familiar in the Pennsylvania Dutch country where the author lives. The iron arms and braces are an interesting innovation which certainly does not detract from this unique piece of furniture.

The turnings and legs are purposely left quite plain, in keeping with the spirit of the whole design. Regular ¾-in. birch dowel rods, with their ends turned down to a diameter of ½ in., are used as rungs on the lower part. The legs swell to their largest diameter about two thirds of the way below the seat, where the front and rear stretchers are joined to them.

While the construction of this piece may seem to be disarmingly simple, several things must be taken into account when it is being assembled.

Because both front and rear legs are slanted, the legs will be from ⅜ to ½-in. farther apart when they enter the holes in the seat than they will be when they have been driven home. This presents a problem in assembling, since this difference must be reckoned with at the time the glue is applied. Be very careful to have the tops of the legs fit the holes in the seat reasonably loose so they may be driven home easily. The top of each leg should have a saw kerf cut to the shoulder of the tenon into which wedges will be driven after the joints are assembled. See Figures 90 and 91.

The ends of the rungs should also be made to fit the holes without being too tight. Furthermore, cut or score-in shallow V grooves along the entire length of the tenons of the end rungs which are to enter their respective holes.

Figure 94 shows a jig which may be clamped to the drill press to bore the holes for rungs at the proper angle.

When the front and rear rungs are being glued into their respective legs, and before the glue has had a chance to dry, fit the legs to their respective holes in the seat, so the legs and rungs are sure to be lined up properly. Do this without putting any glue on the joints at the seat. Glue should only be put on the front and rear rungs, shown in Figure 91, and into the holes to which they are to be

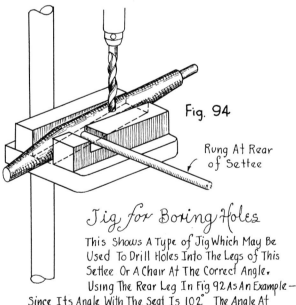

Fig. 94

Rung At Rear of Settee

*Jig for Boring Holes*

This Shows A Type of Jig Which May Be Used To Drill Holes Into The Legs of This Settee Or A Chair At The Correct Angle.
Using The Rear Leg In Fig 92 As An Example— Since Its Angle With The Seat Is 102° The Angle At Which It Is Tilted from The Vertical Is 12°. Thus If A Jig Like This One Tilts The Leg At 12° Along Its Center-Line The Hole Will Be Bored Or Drilled At The Proper Angle. By Placing The Rear Seat Rung In The Hole Which Has Been Drilled For It, The Two Holes May Be Drilled In Correct Relation To Each Other.

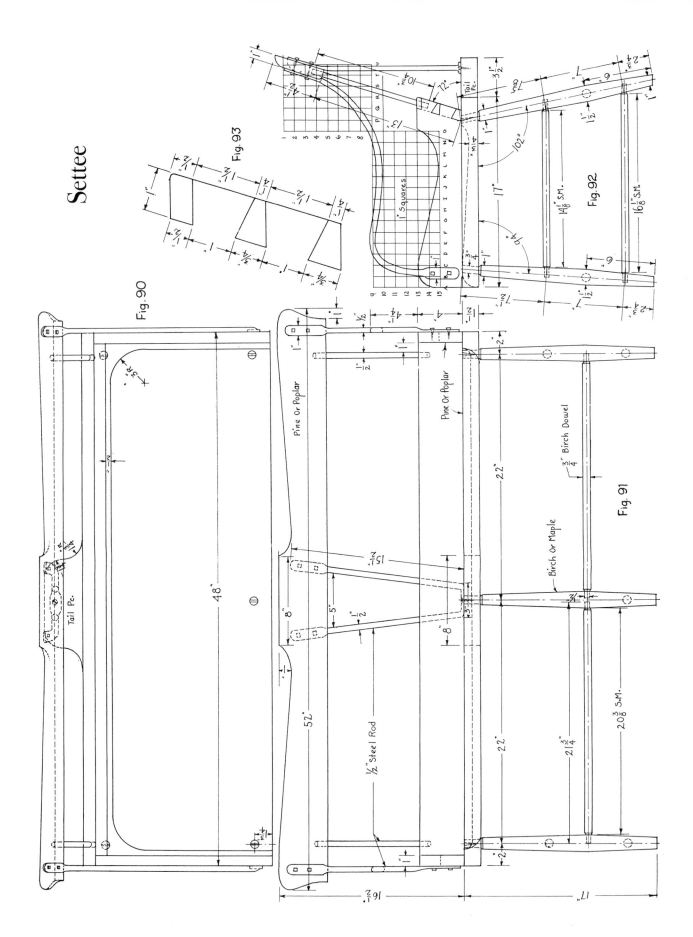

Settee

Fig. 90

Fig. 93

Fig. 92

Fig. 91

52

joined. The rungs going from the front to the rear of the settee should not be put in place at this time.

When the glue has dried in this first operation, remove the legs from the holes in the seat, and then carefully drop some glue into the bottom of each hole to which the five short rungs, two of which are shown in Figure 92, are to be joined. If these holes have been drilled only as deep as the length of the tenon on the rung, the glue which has been put in the bottom of these holes will be forced through the V grooves previously scored into the tenons, as the legs are driven home, and as the clamps placed parallel to each rung pull the joints tightly together.

A word should be said regarding this clamping. Sticks of soft pine, about 2 in. wide, with shallow grooves cut lengthwise, placed on the outside of each leg will prevent the clamps from marring the legs while this is being done.

Next, make the back. Its top edge should be rounded, as shown in Figure 89. When shaping the arms, first flatten the opposite ends so they are at right angles to each other. Drill screw holes. Then make a full-size layout on a board or piece of plywood, and after heating the iron, form the arms as shown in Figure 92.

## BILL OF MATERIAL

| DESCRIPTION | PIECES | DIMENSIONS |
|---|---|---|
| Seat | 1 | 1½ x 20½ x 48 |
| Back | 1 | 1 x 4½ x 52 |
| Front legs | 3 | 1½ x 17¼ |
| Rear legs | 3 | 1½ x 17⅜ |
| Front and rear rungs | 4 | ¾ x 21¾ |
| Lower end rungs and rung between two middle legs | 3 | ¾ x 17⅞ |
| Upper end rungs | 2 | ¾ x 15⅞ |
| Arms (mild steel rods) | 2 | ½ x 27½, approx. |
| Brace at back (mild steel rod) | 1 | ½ x 33, approx. |
| End rods in back (mild steel) | 2 | ½ x 10¾ |

# 16.  Side Chair

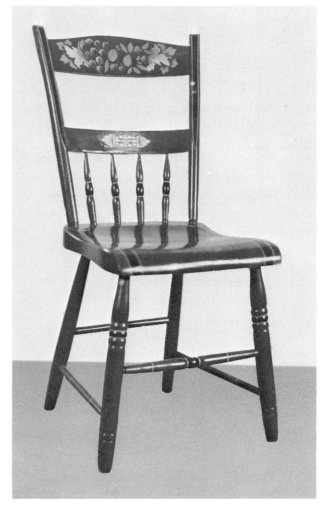

Fig. 95

These stenciled chairs, a type with which several counties in eastern Pennsylvania are richly endowed, are one version of what rather aptly has been termed a "fancy chair." They are probably a country Dutch offspring of an earlier Sheraton-type chair. Whatever their origin, they seem to have been made in great quantity in one form or another because they are still found in profusion around the countryside. A pair of this type belonging to the author are family heirlooms. Their olive-green paint and stenciled decorations blend harmoniously with the natural color of the wood of the other pieces of furniture described in this book.

Chair making is never a simple form of craftsmanship because the pieces which go into the making of a good chair must be shaped and formed to make the chair comfortable to sit on. Even a simple chair, such as this one, with its wooden seat and back, needs to have many of its members curved and shaped to conform to the shape of the human body. Such shaping requires some skill, though not as much, perhaps, as fitting the pieces together. This fitting together needs to be carefully done, so the members will properly brace and support each other and withstand the strains and stresses they are subjected to by the rather hard and constant use given to these pieces of furniture.

First of all, the individual members must be turned or formed to the shape shown in the drawings (Figs. 96 to 102). Then holes must be mortised and bored at correct angles. (Any angles, the degree of which is not specifically given in our drawings, may be taken directly from the drawings with a protractor, since the reduction of a drawing in size for purposes of printing it in a book does not change these angles.) When chairs like these are made in furniture factories, one or

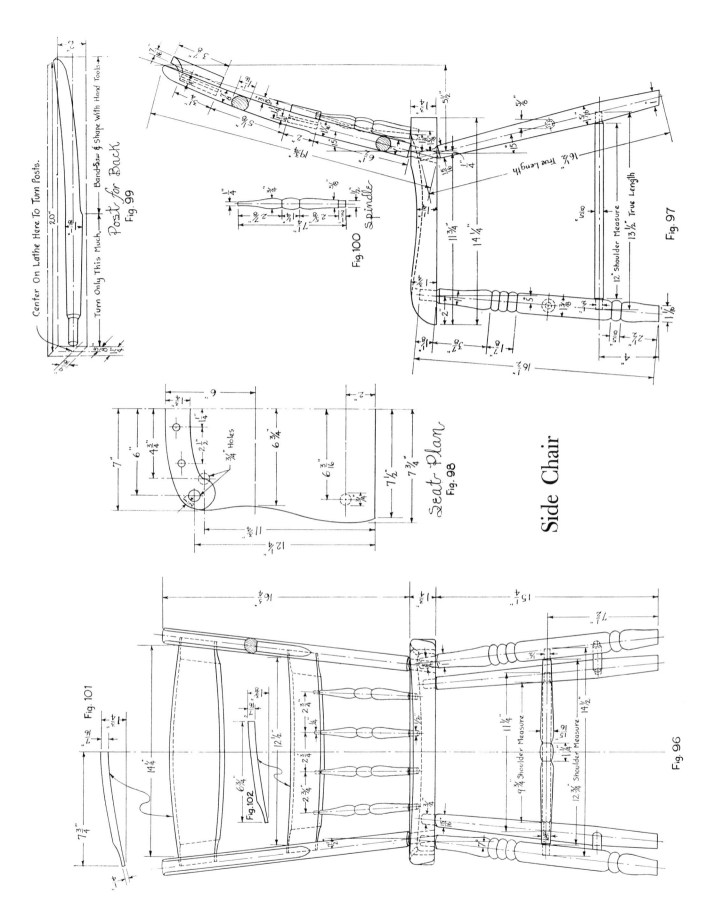

Center On Lathe Here To Turn Posts.

Turn Only This Much,

Band-Saw & Shape With Hand Tools→

Post for Back
Fig. 99

Fig. 100 Spindle

Seat Plan
Fig. 98

Side Chair

Fig. 97

Fig. 96

Fig. 101

Fig. 102

55

more sample chairs are first painstakingly constructed by an expert, and then, from these, the boring angles are determined, and jigs and boring-machine setups are made to insure accuracy and uniformity. Home and school shop facilities, of course, seldom permit such elaborate preparation. If, however, painstaking care is exercised in following the directions given in our drawings, even a person with average skill will find it possible to build such a chair.

In Figure 99, one method is shown of forming the back posts without having to steam and bend the stock. If facilities for steaming and bending these parts are available, the posts may first be turned; then steamed, bent, and cut to shape, as shown. In such case the turning need be only 1 1/16 in. in diameter for the entire length of the post, except the tenon at its base, which is 3/4 in. in diameter.

The directions for boring holes in the seat on a drill press given in making the occasional table in Chapter 4 should be referred to before work is started on this chair. A jig for boring holes in legs similar to these for the rungs is shown in Figure 94, Chapter 15. With these instructions to guide you, the job should not be too difficult.

No directions for stenciling will be given here. Good books are available on this subject. The chairs may be stained, varnished, and rubbed down. Or they may be enameled, and let go at that.

**BILL OF MATERIAL**

| DESCRIPTION | PIECES | DIMENSIONS |
|---|---|---|
| Seat (Poplar) | 1 | 1 3/4 x 15 1/2 x 14 1/4 |
| Front legs (maple) | 2 | 1 3/8 x 16 1/2 |
| Back legs (maple) | 2 | 1 5/16 x 16 1/2 |
| Back posts (maple) | 2 | 1 1/4 x 2 x 20 Size before cutting to shape. See Figure 99. |
| Upper stretcher in back (maple) | 1 | 1 3/4 x 3 7/8 x 15 1/2 Size before cutting to shape. See Figure 101. |
| Lower stretcher in back (maple) | 1 | 1 3/8 x 2 x 13 1/2 Size before cutting to shape. See Figure 102. |
| Front rung (maple) | 1 | 15/16 x 14 1/2 |
| Rear rung (maple or birch) | 1 | 5/8 x 11 1/4 |
| Side rungs (maple or birch) | 2 | 5/8 x 13 1/2 |
| Spindles (maple) | 4 | 3/4 x 7 1/4 See Figure 100. |

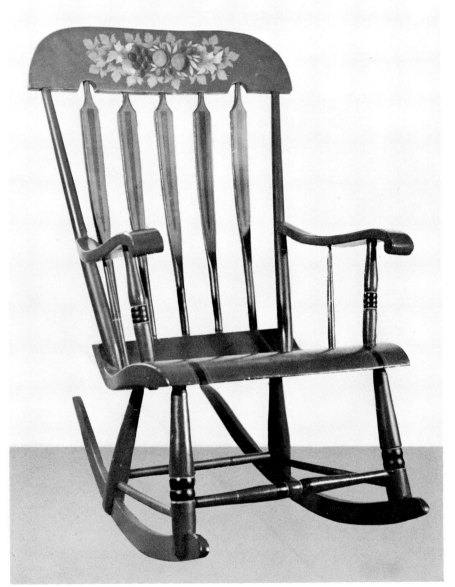

Fig. 103

Since everyone likes to sit in a comfortable rocker, and since Boston rockers are about as comfortable as any chair with a wooden seat can be, the author decided to include one in this book. The one shown in Figure 103 has been in the author's family as long as he can remember, but had become almost a total derelict prior to its restoration about a year before this book was written. The restoration re-quired two new arms, a new rocker, a new splat, and extensive repairs to the seat and other members. The stenciling is on an olive-green background to match the color of the side chairs described in Chapter 16.

As was indicated in the previous chapter, chair making is never a simple operation. There is hardly a straight line on a chair of this kind. Conse-

57

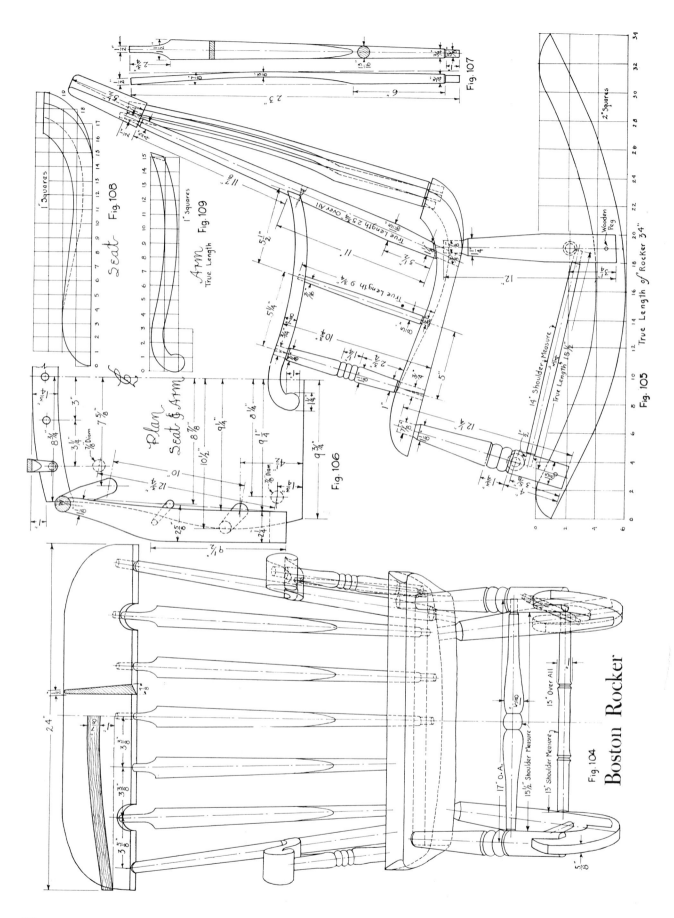

Fig. 107

1" Squares

Seat  Fig. 108

Arm  Fig. 109
True Length

Plan
Seat & Arm

Fig. 106

1" Squares

True Length 25¾" Over All

True Length 9 ¾"

2" Squares

Wooden Peg

True Length of Rocker 34"

14" Shoulder Measure

True Length 15½"

Fig. 105

17" O.A.

15½" Shoulder Measure

15" Over All

15" Shoulder Measure

Fig. 104

## Boston Rocker

quently, most layouts for chairs of this kind must begin with a center line. Boring the holes must be carefully done, and at the proper angles, so the members may be properly fitted together. In the drawings shown in Figures 104 to 106, no angles have been dimensioned; they may be taken directly from the drawings with a protractor.

It should be noted, when making the seat, that it is hollowed out in both directions, as indicated by dotted lines in Figures 104 and 105. The high section of the seat at the back where the splats are joined to it is glued to the top of the plank from which most of the seat is formed.

The splats in the back are curved considerably, the pieces for them being turned down from ⅞ in. in thickness to ⅜ in. to fit the curve of the back, and also to make them springy enough for greater comfort.

Directions for making the chair, other than those we have just given above, would be quite similar to those we have already given for building the settee in Chapter 15 and the side chair in Chapter 16; for this reason we suggest that the instructions given in those chapters be read before starting work on this project.

### BILL OF MATERIAL

| DESCRIPTION | PIECES | DIMENSIONS |
|---|---|---|
| Seat (poplar) | 1 | 2 x 21 x 19 |
| Strip to be glued on top of seat at the back. | 1 | 1½ x 17½ x 4¼ |
| Front legs (maple) | 2 | 1⅝ x 12¼ |
| Rear legs (maple) | 2 | 2 x 12 |
| Rockers (maple or hickory) | 2 | ⅝ x 6 x 34 |
| Posts in back (maple) | 2 | 1$\frac{5}{16}$ x 25¾ |
| Front arm supports (maple) | 2 | 1⅛ x 10¾ |
| Middle arm support spindles | 2 | ⅝ x 9¾ |
| Back splats (maple or hickory) | 5 | ⅞ x 1½ x 23 |
| Top of back (maple) | 1 | 1⅞ x 5½ x 24 |
| Arms (maple) | 2 | 2½ x 2⅝ x 15⅜ |
| Front rung under seat (maple) | 1 | 1⅝ x 17 |
| Back rung under seat (maple or birch) | 1 | 1 x 15 |
| Side rungs above rockers (maple or birch) | 2 | ¾ x 15½ |

# 18. Windsor Arm Chair

Windsor chairs, such as the one shown in Figure 110, are hard to surpass for appearance and comfort. Though contemporary designers have tried their best to improve upon this type of chair, the author has seen none which from the standpoint of style and comfort could be called superior to a really well-designed Windsor. In studying these chairs in museums and in private collections, the student is astonished by the great variety inculcated in the design.

White pine is the wood most frequently used for seats on old chairs of this type, though other woods such as poplar, maple, and birch, are to be found. Seats for these chairs must be carefully formed for comfort. Templates and hand tools are used in the final stages of forming the really good ones. In factories, of course, where this type of chair is built in quantity, the preliminary forming is done on machines. The grain in the seat runs from side to side, and not from front to back.

In building this chair, close attention should be paid to the quality and sharpness of the forming on the turned members. Curves bulge suddenly, and are left sharp and crisp at terminals. This gives character to the finished production. See Figures 114 and 115.

Making the hand-carved scrolls on the arms should be given careful attention, for they add considerably to the beauty of the chair. See Figures 113 and 116.

Before building this chair, read the instructions for building the settee, Chapter 15, and the side chair, Chapter 16, where many of the instructions needed to build this chair will be found.

## BILL OF MATERIAL

| DESCRIPTION | PIECES | DIMENSIONS |
|---|---|---|
| Seat (white pine) | 1 | 2 x 18 x 21 |
| Legs (maple) | 4 | 1¾ x 19 |
| Arm supports (maple) | 2 | 1⅝ x 13 |
| Medial stretcher (maple) | 1 | 1⅞ x 18 |
| End rungs (maple) | 2 | 1⅞ x 15 |
| Spindles in back (maple or hickory) | 15 | ⅞ x 12 |
| Arms (maple) | 2 | ⅞ x 6¾ x 21¼ |
| Small blocks to be glued under ends of arm where they are carved | 2 | ½ x 2⅝ x 1¼ |

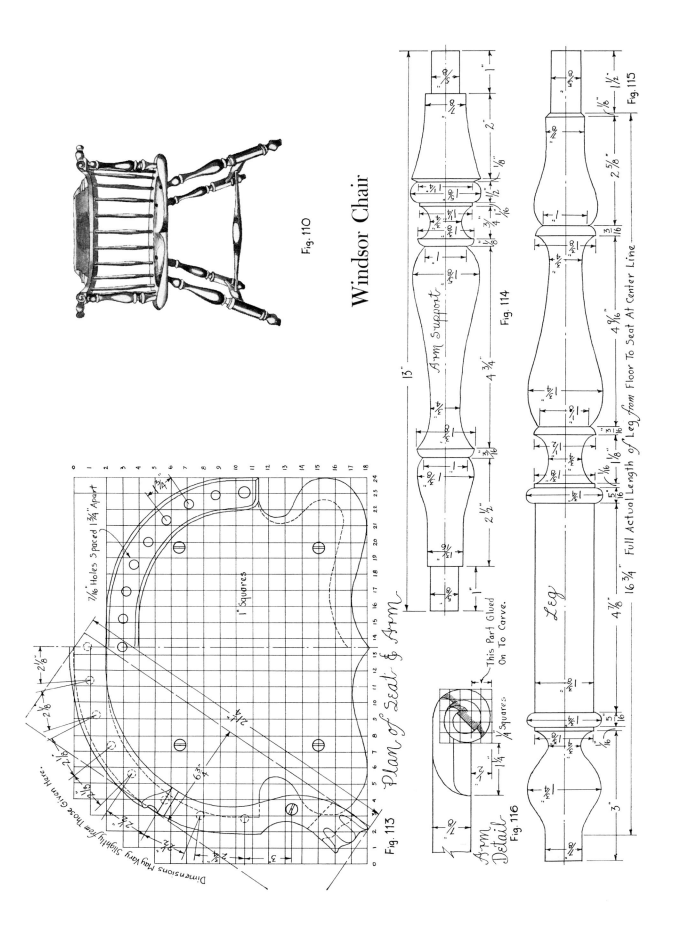

Fig. 11O

# Windsor Chair

Fig. 113 — Plan of Seat & Arm

7/16 Holes Spaced 1¾" Apart

1" Squares

Dimensions May Vary Slightly from Those Given Here.

Arm Support — Fig. 114

13"

Leg — Fig. 115

16¾"  Full Actual Length of Leg from Floor To Seat At Center Line

4 9/16

Arm Detail — Fig. 116

This Part Glued On To Carve.

¼ Squares

# Windsor Arm Chair

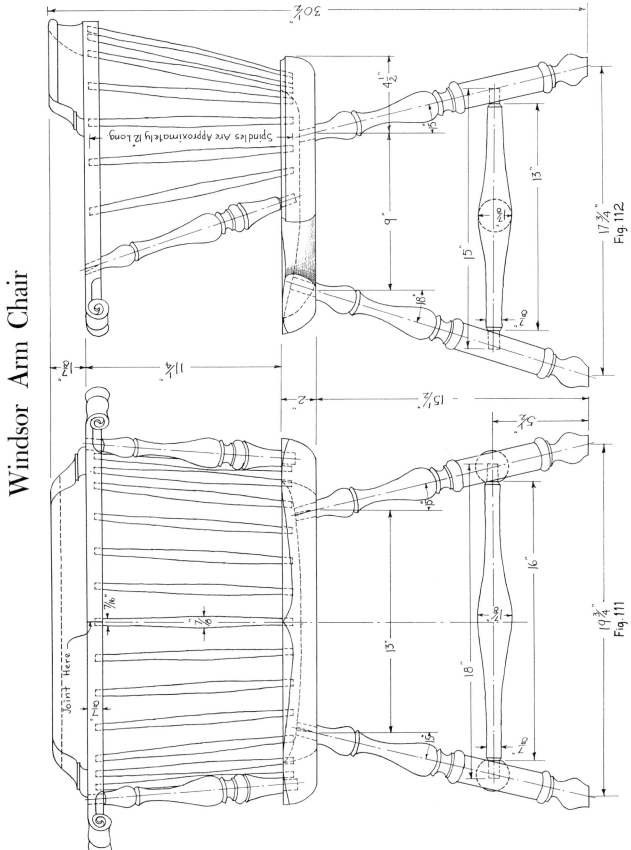

Spindles Are Approximately 12" Long

Joint Here

Fig. 112

Fig. 111

30½"

17¾"

4½"

15°

13"

15"

9"

18°

⁷⁄₈"

⁷⁄₈"

8½"

11¼"

2"

15½"

5½"

15°

16"

13"

18"

15°

⁷⁄₈"

⁷⁄₈"

19¾"

⁷⁄₁₆"

⁷⁄₈"

⁷⁄₈"

Fig. 117

## BILL OF MATERIAL

| DESCRIPTION | PIECES | DIMENSIONS |
|---|---|---|
| **Wood, Yellow Poplar** | | |
| Ends | 2 | ¾ x 10¼ x 76 |
|  | 2 | ¾ x 4¼ x 20⅝ |
| Stiles (A) | 2 | ¾ x 1⅝ x 54⅝ |
| Stiles (B) | 2 | ¾ x 1⅝ x 20⅝ |
| Top rail (C) | 1 | ¾ x 2¼ x 24¾ |
| Rail (D) | 1 | ¾ x 1¼ x 24¾ |
| Rail (E) | 1 | ¾ x 2½ x 24¾ |
| Top (F) | 1 | ¾ x 13¼ x 29¾ |
| Front part, feet (G) | 1 | ¾ x 3¼ x 27¼ |
| End parts, feet (H) | 2 | ¾ x 3¼ x 16 |
| Rear part, feet (I) | 1 | ¾ x 4⅛ x 24¼ |
| Table-board (J) | 1 | ¾ x 16¼ x 27¾ (See Fig. 122.) |
| Gunstock holder (K) | 1 | ¾ x 10¼ x 24¼ (See Fig. 122.) |
| Gun-barrel holder (L) | 1 | ¾ x 2 x 24¼ (See Fig. 118.) |
| Floor (M) | 1 | ¾ x 14¼ x 24¼ |
| Shelf (N) | 1 | ¾ x 14¼ x 24¼ |
| Upper door stiles (T) | 2 | ¾ x 2¼ x 52 |
| Upper door rails, upper and lower (U) | 2 | ¾ x 2¼ x 21⅛ |
| Upper door rails (V) | 3 | ¾ x 1 x 21⅛ |
| Upper door mullions (W) | 4 | ¾ x 1 x 11⅝ |
| Back (plywood) (X) | 1 | ¼ x 25 x 72¼ |
| Crown molding around top: approx. 60 in. (see Fig. 123) | | |
| Quarter-round glass molding (see Fig. 120) | | |
| Strips at end of table-board (O) | 2 | ¾ x 1 x 16½ (See Fig. 122.) |
| Strips under table-board (P) | 2 | ¾ x ¾ x 14¼ (See Fig. 122.) |
| Lower door stiles (Q) | 2 | ¾ x 2¼ x 15⅝ (See Figs. 118 and 121.) |
| Lower door rails (R) | 2 | ¾ x 2¼ x 21⅛ (See Figs. 118 and 121.) |
| Lower door panel (S) | 1 | ¾ x 19⅜ x 11⅞ |

For the person who has several presentable looking guns the cabinet shown in Figure 117 is an ideal and handsome one in which to display them to good advantage.

Except for making the doors, the construction of this gun cabinet is quite simple. The ends are glued up first, planed and properly sanded, as shown in Figure 124. Rabbet the rear edge for the back. Next, make and fasten the rails (P) (as in Fig. 122). Make the shelf (N), the floor (M), and table-board (J). These pieces may now be assembled with wood screws and finishing nails, as shown in Figures 119 and 122. Make the top, and rabbet its back edge. Fasten the top with 6-penny finishing nails. Make a frame, consisting

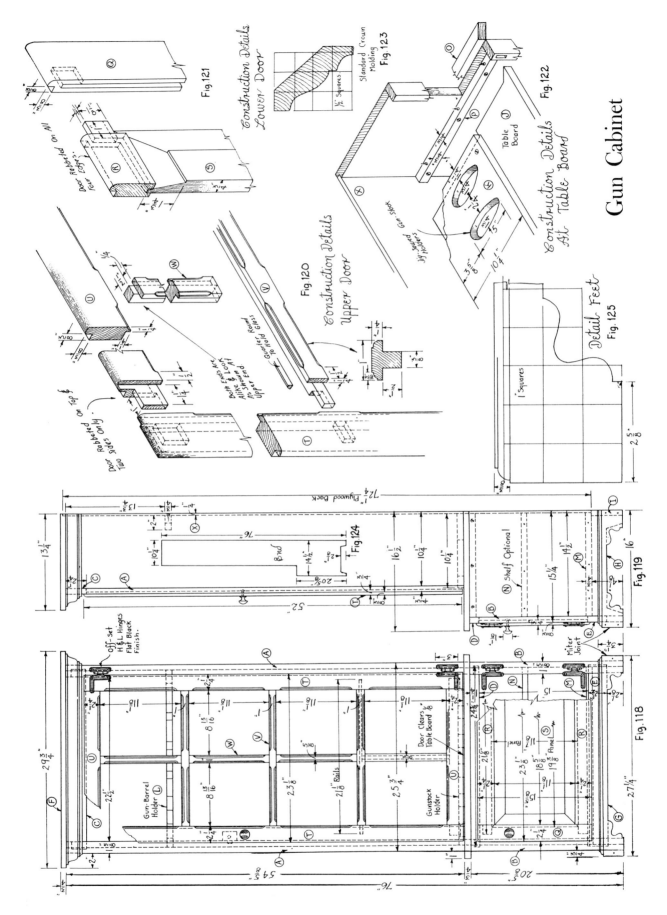

Gun Cabinet

64

of rail (C) and stiles (A), and nail these to the ends with 4-penny finishing nails. Make the lower frame consisting of stiles (B) and rails (D) and (E), and nail this to the ends.

Cut the plywood back and nail it from the rear with 2-penny lath nails.

Make the gunstock holder (K), as shown in Figure 122. Screw it fast to the table-board. Make the gun-barrel holder (L) and fasten it with small screws from the rear of the cabinet, as shown in Figure 119.

Make the strips (O) to finish off the edge of the table-board, and run it to the rear edge of the ends on the outside, as shown in Figure 119.

Make the feet according to the pattern in Figure 125. The feet are mitered together at the front corners and nailed to the lower rail (E) and the ends with 4-penny finishing nails. Make and nail piece (I) to each end, as shown in Figure 119.

The crown molding at the top of the cabinet is a standard stock molding which may be bought cheaply at almost any lumberyard. It usually comes in white pine, a wood which may be used with poplar.

The lower door differs from the doors we have described in the chapter on the built-in corner cupboard in only one respect: it is rabbeted on the edges to form a rounded lip, as shown in Figure 121. Panels are raised in the same way as those described in Chapter 5 for the paneled wastebasket.

The upper door will be the most difficult member of this project to build. However, if rails and stiles are mortised, tenoned, joined, and glued together first without rabbeting the outside rails and stiles on the outside edges, the rest of the work may be done after these members have been assembled. The rabbeting on the inside of these members must be done before assembling, of course, as must the rabbeting on the narrow rails. The mullions may be joined to the rails after this with a bit of glue and very thin (#19 or 20 brads). The three outside edges of the door are rabbeted next, as indicated in Figures 118, 119, and 120.

The molding around each pane of glass may be cut on a shaper after the door has been completely assembled. Glass is fastened on the inside by means of narrow quarter-round molding, as shown in Figure 120.

Locks may be put on the doors as indicated in Figure 118, and as shown in Figure 117.

To fasten the doors to the cabinet, use 3-in. H and L offset hinges, which will fit perfectly if the doors are made as shown in the drawings.

# 20.  Large Gun Cabinet

Fig. 126

Anyone who would like to have an attractive gun cabinet, slightly larger than the one just described in Chapter 19, might want to build the one shown in Figure 126. Plain glass in the upper doors to show off a collection of guns, and beautifully paneled doors below, make this cabinet a showpiece in anyone's home.

Except for the fact that the doors in this cabinet are flush with the faces of the doorframes and have large single panes of glass, the construction of the two cabinets is about the same. Before beginning the work on this piece, it might be well to read the instructions given for making the cabinet in Chapter 19.

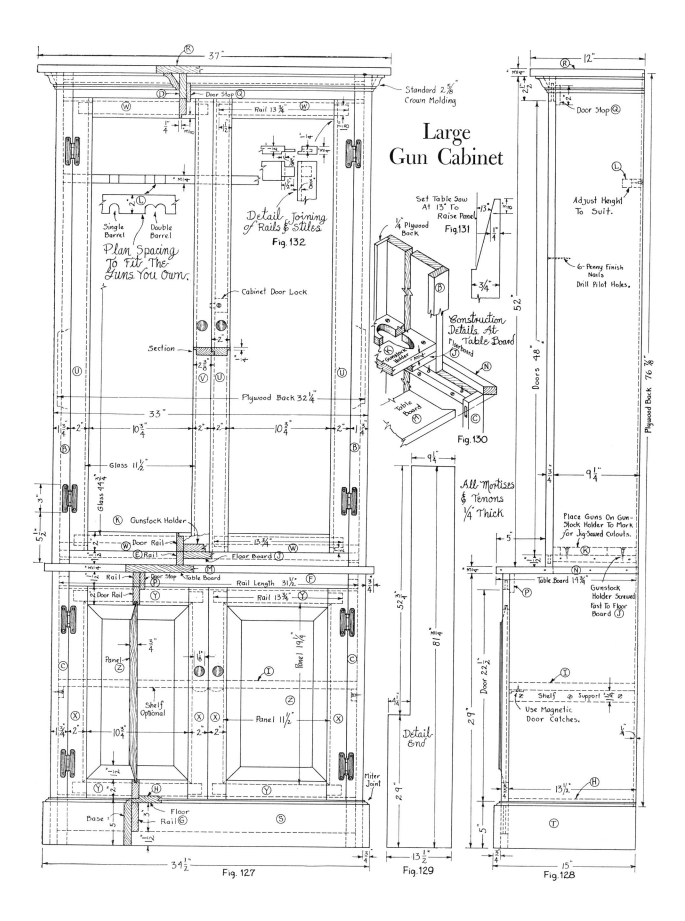

Large Gun Cabinet

Standard 2 5/8" Crown Molding

Single Barrel    Double Barrel

Plan Spacing To Fit The Guns You Own.

Detail Joining of Rails & Stiles
Fig. 132

Set Table Saw At 13° To Raise Panel.
Fig. 131

Cabinet Door Lock

Section

Plywood Back 32¼"

Construction Details At Table Board
Fig. 130

All Mortises & Tenons ¼" Thick

Adjust Height To Suit.

6-Penny Finish Nails Drill Pilot Holes.

Glass 11½"

Gunstock Holder

Door Rail
Rail

Floor Board J

Door Stop    Table Board

Rail Length 31½"

Door Rail

Rail 13¾

Panel 19¼

Panel 11½

Shelf Optional

Miter Joint

Base    Floor Rail G

Detail End

Place Guns On Gun-Stock Holder To Mark for Jig-Sawed Cutouts.

Table Board 13¾

Gunstock Holder Screwed Fast To Floor Board J

Use Magnetic Door Catches.

Shelf Support

Fig. 127

Fig. 129

Fig. 128

Ends are glued up in the same manner, as shown in Figure 129. Paneled doors are made in the same way as on the other cabinet. Figure 131 shows the angle to set the table saw for raising the panels.

It should be noted here that the floor of the lower part is rabbeted along the front edge to make a doorstop, as shown at (H) in Figure 127. It should also be pointed out that the upper doors have an overlapping rabbeted joint where they meet, as shown in the section at (V) in Figure 127, and for this reason this one stile is ⅜ in. wider than the other three.

Except for these few notations we believe the similarity of construction makes it unnecessary to repeat the instructions already given for making the smaller gun cabinet. By studying the drawings (Figs. 127 to 132) and the photograph (Fig. 126) most of the things that will need to be done should become self-evident.

## BILL OF MATERIAL

| DESCRIPTION | PIECES | DIMENSIONS |
|---|---|---|
| Ends (A) | 2 | ¾ x 9¼ x 81¾ |
| | 2 | ¾ x 4¼ x 29 |
| Stiles, upper part (B) | 2 | ¾ x 1¾ x 52 |
| Stiles, lower part (C) | 2 | ¾ x 1¾ x 29 |
| Rail (D) | 1 | ¾ x 2½ x 31½ |
| Rail (E) | 1 | ¾ x 1½ x 31½ |
| Rail (F) | 1 | ¾ x 1½ x 31½ |
| Rail (G) | 1 | ¾ x 3 x 31½ |
| Floor (H) | 1 | ¾ x 14 x 31½ |
| Shelf (I) | 1 | ¾ x 13¼ x 31½ |
| Floorboard (J) | 1 | ¾ x 9 x 31½ |
| Gunstock holder (K) | 1 | ¾ x 9 x 31½ |
| Gun-barrel holder (L) | 1 | ¾ x 2 x 31½ |
| Table-board (M) | 1 | ¾ x 14¾ x 34½ |
| Strips at end of table-board (N) | 2 | ¾ x ¾ x 15 |
| Shelf supports (O) | 2 | ¾ x 1¼ x 13¼ |
| Doorstop (P) | 1 | ½ x 1¾ x 31½ |
| Doorstop (Q) | 1 | ½ x 2 x 31½ |
| Top (R) | 1 | ¾ x 12 x 37 |
| Front of base (S) | 1 | ¾ x 5 x 34½ |
| Ends of base (T) | 2 | ¾ x 5 x 15 |
| Door stiles (U) | 3 | ¾ x 2 x 48 |
| Door stile (V) | 1 | ¾ x 2⅜ x 48 |
| Door rails (W) | 4 | ¾ x 2 x 13¾ |
| Door stiles (X) | 4 | ¾ x 2 x 22½ |
| Door rails (Y) | 4 | ¾ x 2 x 13¾ |
| Door panels (Z) | 2 | ¾ x 11½ x 19¼ |
| Standard crown molding | 1 | 2⅝ x 60 approx. |

Fig. 133

Everyone who has a home workshop will wish to have a good place to store his tools. The tool cabinet shown in Figure 133 not only provides ample and convenient space for tools and accessories, but it is an attractive piece of furniture, and will certainly dress up any home workshop.

Among other things, it displays the tools in an attractive manner, behind sliding glass doors, and its drawers and cupboards provide a considerable amount of additional storage room.

To build the cabinet, first glue up the ends (Fig. 137), partitions, and floor (Fig. 138). The ends

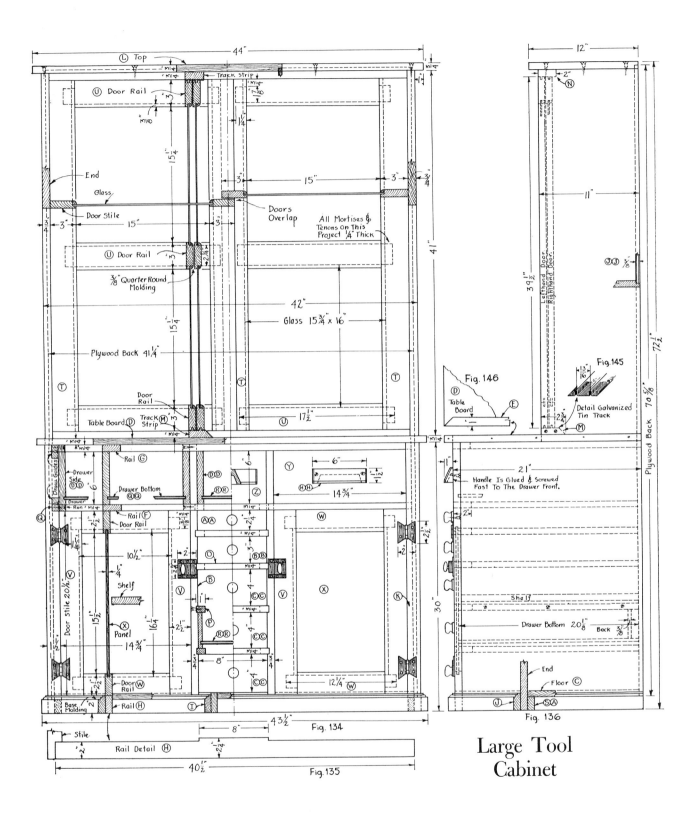

Large Tool
Cabinet

Fig. 134

Fig. 135

Fig. 136

Fig. 146

Fig. 145

70

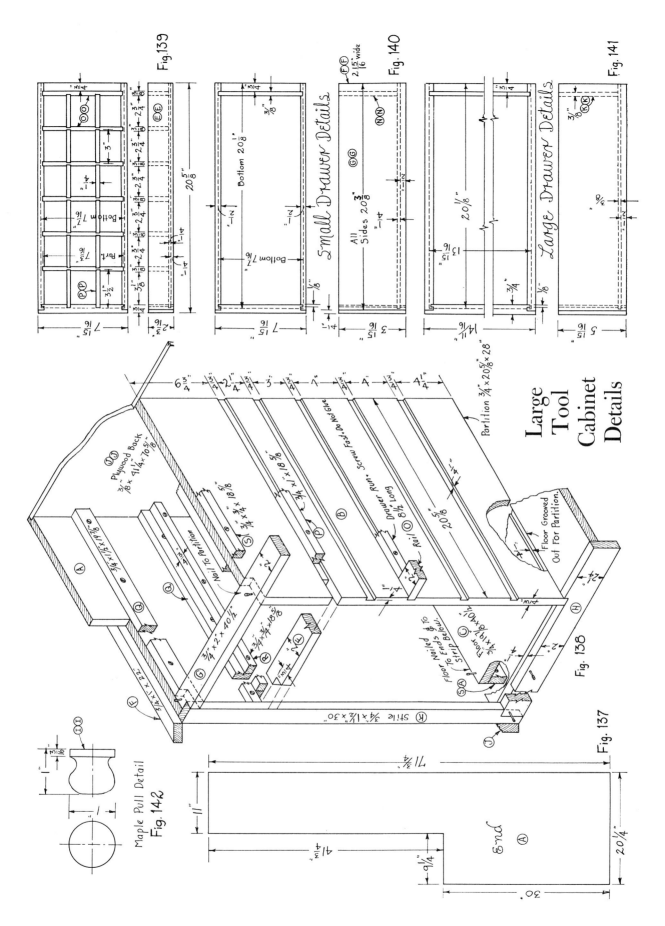

Fig.139

Fig.140

Small Drawer Details

Fig.141

Large Drawer Details

Large
Tool
Cabinet
Details

Fig. 138

Fig. 137

Maple Pull Detail
Fig. 142

have ⅜ by ⅜-in. rabbeted back edges, to which the plywood back may be nailed without its edges showing.

The floor is grooved out ¼ in. deep for the partitions to fit into, and the partitions are also grooved on one side to support the drawer runs and front rails, as shown in Figure 138. The partitions are notched out at the top for the two long rails (*F*) and (*G*), which run from one end of the cabinet to the other.

Once these grooves and notches have been cut, the drawer runs and drawer glides may be fastened with wood screws, as shown in Figure 138. Also screw on strips (*S-A*) at the bottom of the ends to which you will later nail the ends of the floor. An extra one of these strips may be nailed under the center of the floor to help support it if this is found to be necessary.

Now assemble ends (*A*), partitions (*B*), floor (*C*), and rails (*F*) and (*G*) in that order. The ends of (*F*) and (*G*) are also notched to allow the two stiles (*K*) to be fitted flush with their front edges when later these are nailed to the ends. Partitions may be glued to the floor grooves, but several wood screws will help to keep them in place. Drawer runs should not be glued to the grooves in the partitions because when the partitions expand or contract, as they will in different seasons of the year, a glued-in run will either split or warp the partitions. Instead of glue, two or even three wood screws may be used for securing the runs.

Next, make stiles (*K*) and rail (*H*), and nail these to the assembled parts. Please note the shape of (*H*) in Figure 135. The base moldings (*I*) and (*J*) may be made at this time and nailed around the bottom.

Make and fasten the plywood back (*J-J*) next. This must be run up high enough at the top so that later it may be nailed fast to the rabbeted back edge of the top (*L*). This top is fastened to the ends with wood screws only after the sliding doors have been made and put in place.

Drawers and doors for the lower part may now be made and fitted. Figures 139 to 141 give dimensions and details for making these. For greatest ease they should be fitted before the table-board is put on. Figure 144 shows how the fronts of the drawers are cut for joining them to the drawer sides. Such joints insure a sturdy drawer, and sturdiness is essential in a drawer which is to hold tools of considerable weight.

## BILL OF MATERIAL

| DESCRIPTION | PIECES | DIMENSIONS |
|---|---|---|
| Ends (A) | 2 | ¾ x 11 x 71¾ |
| | 2 | ¾ x 9¼ x 30 (See Fig. 137.) |
| Partitions (B) | 2 | ¾ x 20⅝ x 28 |
| Floorboard (C) | 1 | ¾ x 19⅞ x 40½ |
| Table-board (D) | 1 | ¾ x 21⅝ x 44 |
| Strips at ends of table-board (E) | 2 | ¾ x 1 x 22 |
| Rail below table-board (G) | 1 | ¾ x 2 x 40½ |
| Rail below large drawers (F) | 1 | ¾ x 2 x 40½ |
| Rail below doors (H) | 1 | ¾ x 2¼ x 40½ (See Fig. 135.) |
| Front base molding (I) | 1 | ¾ x 2 x 43½ |
| Base molding at ends (J) | 2 | ¾ x 2 x 21¾ |
| Stiles (K) | 2 | ¾ x 1½ x 30 |
| Top (L) | 1 | ¾ x 12 x 44 |
| Lower track strip (M) | 1 | ¾ x 2¾ x 40½ |
| Upper track strip (N) | 1 | ¾ x 2 x 40½ |
| Rail between small drawers (O) | 4 | ¾ x 2 x 8½ |
| Drawer runs (P) | 10 | ¾ x 1 x 18⅝ |
| Drawer guides (Q) | 4 | ¾ x 1½ x 19⅞ |
| Drawer runs (R) | 4 | ¾ x ¾ x 18⅝ (See Fig. 138.) |
| Strips to fasten partitions to table-board (S) | 4 | ¾ x ¾ x 18⅝ |
| Strips to hold up floor-board (S-A) | 2 | ¾ x 1½ x 19¾ |
| Stiles for upper doors (T) | 4 | ¾ x 3 x 39½ |
| Rails for upper doors (U) | 6 | ¾ x 3 x 17½ |
| Stiles for lower doors (V) | 4 | ¾ x 2½ x 20½ |
| Rails for lower doors (W) | 4 | ¾ x 2½ x 12¼ |
| Panels for lower doors (X) | 2 | ¼ x 10½ x 16¼ |
| Large drawer fronts (Y) | 2 | ¾ x 5 15/16 x 14 11/16 |
| Drawer front (Z) | 1 | ¾ x 5 15/16 x 7 15/16 |
| Drawer front (A-A) | 1 | ¾ x 2 3/16 x 7 15/16 |
| Drawer front (B-B) | 1 | ¾ x 2 15/16 x 7 15/16 |
| Drawer fronts (C-C) | 3 | ¾ x 3 15/16 x 7 15/16 |
| Drawer sides (D-D) | 6 | ¾ x 5 15/16 x 20⅜ |
| Drawer sides (E-E) | 2 | ½ x 2 3/16 x 20⅜ |
| Drawer sides (F-F) | 2 | ½ x 2 15/16 x 20⅜ |
| Drawer sides (G-G) | 6 | ½ x 3 15/16 x 20⅜ |
| Handles (H-H) | 3 | 1 x 1½ x 6 |
| Drawer pulls (I-I) | 5 | 1 x 1 |
| Back (plywood) (J-J) | 1 | ⅜ x 41¼ x 70⅝ |
| Drawer backs (K-K) | 2 | ⅜ x 5 1/16 x 13 15/16 |
| Drawer backs (L-L), top middle drawer | 1 | ⅜ x 5 1/16 x 7 3/16 |
| Drawer back, 3-in. drawer, (M-M) | 1 | ⅜ x 2 3/16 x 7 3/16 |
| Drawer backs, 4-in. drawers (N-N) | 3 | ⅜ x 3 3/16 x 7 3/16 |
| Partitions and back, small drawer (O-O) | 6 | ⅜ x 1 11/16 x 7 3/16 |
| Partitions (P-P) | 12 | ¼ x 1 11/16 x 3½ |
| Drawer bottoms, large drawers (plywood) (Q-Q) | 2 | ¼ x 13 15/16 x 20⅛ |
| Drawer bottoms, all middle drawers (plywood) (R-R) | 6 | ¼ x 7 7/16 x 20⅛ |

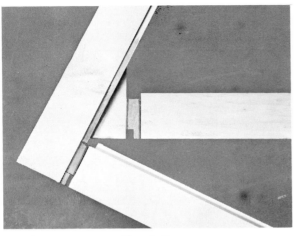

Fig. 143

The table-board may be made and fastened next. Notice that a miter is cut on its ends at the front to permit strip (E) to be joined to it (Fig. 146).

Now make track strips (M) and (N). Galvanized iron tracks were made for the cabinet shown. Since these must be at least partly formed on a long bar folder to get them straight, they should be taken to the nearest tinsmith who can do this job best. See the detail shown in Figure 145. They should be drilled and countersunk for small flathead wood screws, and then secured to the track strips (M) and (N). Some of the screws which hold them in place may be put right under the doors without interfering with their sliding if the heads are properly countersunk. A little graphite or wax on the tracks will make the doors slide more easily.

Figure 143 shows the construction of the joints on these sliding doors. For easy replacement, the glass should be fitted into rabbets cut on the inside edge of each rail and stile, necessitating long- and short-shoulder mortise-and-tenon joints. The door in front (Fig. 143) shows the inside of the joint while that in the rear shows the outside of the joint and the long side of the tenon. The tenon on the outside of the door must be as much longer than its short side as the rabbet is wide. The joints are glued and pinned with hardwood pegs.

When the doors have been assembled, a groove ⅛ in. wide is cut at the top and the bottom of each to accommodate the tracks. Clearance of about 1/16 in. between doors should be provided when cutting these grooves. After the grooves are made the doors may be fitted to the tracks, and the strips to which the metal tracks have been fastened may be screwed to the cabinet. Track strip (N) should be fastened to the top (L), and then top (L) should be fastened with wood screws to the ends, as shown in Figure 136.

The finish put on this tool cabinet was a light burnt-umber oil stain, followed with a sealer, and then several coats of varnish. The final coat was a satin-gloss varnish.

Fig. 144

# 22. Tool Cabinet to Hang on Wall

Fig. 147

This tool cabinet, a smaller, simpler model than the one in Figure 133, is built to be hung on the wall, above or near a workbench, as shown in Figure 147.

By having it so close to where work is being done, each tool may be easily reached when needed, and may just as easily be replaced on its rack when not in use. Thus the surface of the workbench can be kept unlittered.

Glass panels in the doors help keep dampness and dirt from the tools, and the individual racks may be planned so any tool may be removed or replaced without disturbing other tools, as shown in Figure 147.

The construction of the doors is almost identical to that of the doors in the large tool cabinet described in the previous chapter. However, the doors in this cabinet (Figs. 148 and 149) have tongues on top and bottom, which slide in grooves cut into a track at the top, and into a shelf at the bottom. These are carefully fitted and made to slide freely before the top is fastened to the ends

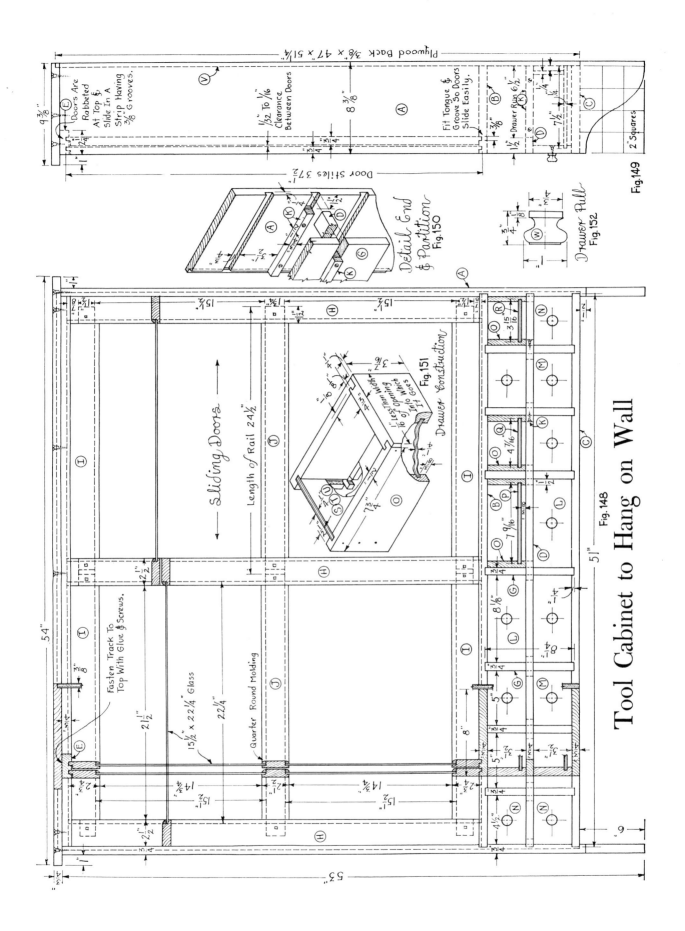

Doors Are Rabbeted At Top & Slide In A Strip Having 3/8 Grooves.

Plywood Back 3/8" x 47" x 51¼"

1/32 To 1/16 Clearance Between Doors

8 3/8"

Fit Tongue & Groove So Doors Slide Easily.

Drawer Run 6½

Door Stiles 37½

Fig. 149

2" Squares

Detail End & Partition Fig. 150

Drawer Pull Fig. 152

Sliding Doors

Length of Rail 24½"

1" Less Than Width To Of Opening Into Which It Goes

Drawer Construction Fig. 151

Fasten Track To Top With Glue & Screws.

15½ x 22¼ Glass

22¼"

Quarter Round Molding

54

53"

6"

51"

Tool Cabinet to Hang on Wall

Fig. 148

and the plywood back. For construction details of doors like these, see Figure 143, in the preceding chapter, as well as Figures 148 and 149 in this one.

Drawer construction is also the same as for the drawers on the larger tool cabinet. See Figures 151 and 144.

The method of making and joining the parts for the lower section, which holds the drawers, is shown in Figure 150. White pine was used to build both these tool cabinets.

**BILL OF MATERIAL**

| DESCRIPTION | PIECES | DIMENSIONS |
|---|---|---|
| Ends (A) | 2 | 3/4 x 8 3/8 x 53 |
| Shelf (B) | 1 | 3/4 x 8 x 51 |
| Bottom (C) | 1 | 3/4 x 8 x 51 |
| Strip separating upper and lower drawers (D) | 1 | 3/4 x 1 1/2 x 51 |
| Track strip at top of cabinet (E) | 1 | 3/4 x 2 1/4 x 50 1/2 |
| Top (F) | 1 | 3/4 x 9 3/8 x 54 |
| Partitions (G) | 7 | 3/4 x 8 x 8 1/4 |
| Door stiles (H) | 4 | 3/4 x 2 1/2 x 37 1/2 |
| Upper and lower door rails (I) | 4 | 3/4 x 2 3/4 x 24 1/2 |
| Middle door rails (J) | 2 | 3/4 x 2 1/2 x 24 1/2 |
| Drawer runs (K) | 16 | 1/2 x 3/4 x 6 1/2 |
| Large drawer fronts (L) | 4 | 3/4 x 3 7/16 x 8 1/16 |
| Drawer fronts (M) | 8 | 3/4 x 3 7/16 x 4 15/16 |
| Drawer fronts (N) | 4 | 3/4 x 3 7/16 x 4 7/16 |
| Drawer sides (O) | 32 | 1/2 x 3 7/16 x 7 3/4 |
| Drawer bottoms (plywood) (P) | 4 | 1/4 x 7 1/2 x 7 9/16 |
| Drawer bottoms (plywood) (Q) | 8 | 1/4 x 7 1/2 x 4 7/16 |
| Drawer bottoms (plywood) (R) | 4 | 1/4 x 7 1/2 x 3 15/16 |
| Drawer backs (plywood) (S) | 4 | 1/4 x 2 15/16 x 7 9/16 |
| Drawer backs (plywood) (T) | 8 | 1/4 x 2 15/16 x 4 7/16 |
| Drawer backs (plywood) (U) | 4 | 1/4 x 2 15/16 x 3 15/16 |
| Back of cabinet (plywood) (V) | 1 | 3/8 x 47 x 51 1/4 |
| Drawer pulls (W) | 16 | 1 x 3/4 |

# 23. Desk or Dressing Table

Fig. 153

The fine piece of furniture shown in Figure 153 may be used either as a desk or as a dressing table. If used as a dressing table, a mirror, like the one shown in Figure 162, should be hung above it. The construction of this mirror will be described in the following chapter.

Some of the features which make the design an appropriate one for both purposes are the large table or work surface, plenty of room in the center to sit up close in comfort, and ample drawer space. The pleasing appearance of this design is evident in the illustration.

To make this piece, first glue up the ends (**A**) and (**B**) to go on both sides of the drawer sections; then glue up the back (**D**). On the front edges of (**A**) saw out places for the quarter columns, as shown in Figures 155 and 160. The bottoms of the ends may be cut out to the exact shape of the feet, which are later fastened to them with wood screws from the inside, or they may be cut out to the shape of the dotted lines shown at the bottom of Figure 155. Since the grain of the wood on the feet runs horizontally, and the grain of the wood on the ends runs vertically, the screws

77

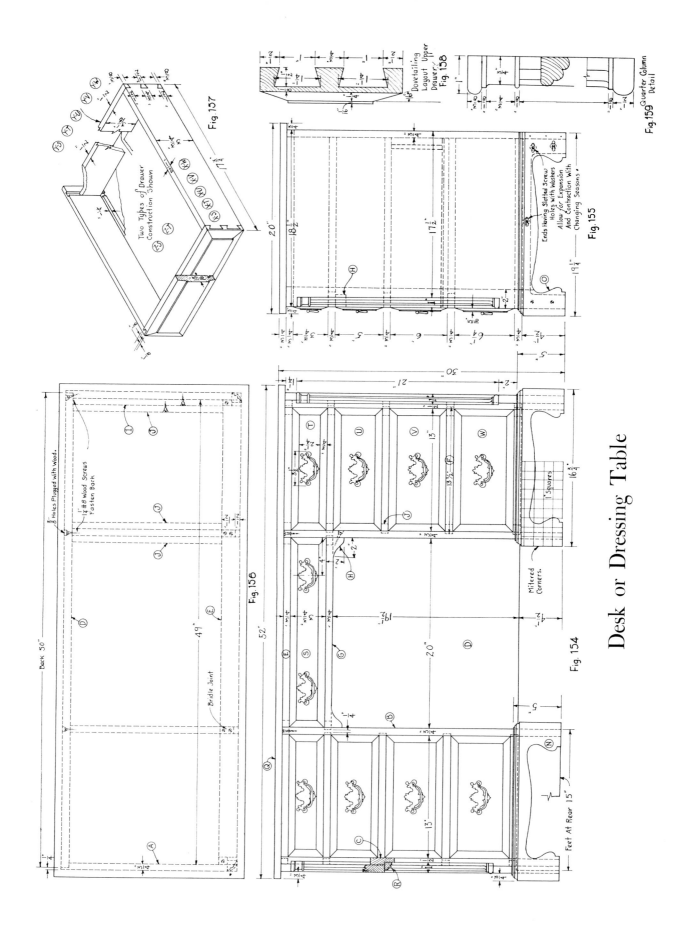

Fig. 157

Two Types of Drawer Construction Shown

Fig. 158
Dovetailing Layout Upper Drawer

Fig.159 Quarter Column Detail

Fig. 155

Ends Having Slotted Screw Holes With Washers Allow For Expansion And Contraction With Changing Seasons.

Fig. 156

3 Holes Plugged With Wood.

1¼ #8 Wood Screws Fasten Back

Back 50"

Bridle Joint

49"

52"

Fig. 154

1 Squares

Mitered Corners.

Feet At Rear 15"

Desk or Dressing Table

at the middle and rear are passed through slotted holes to allow for expansion or contraction with the change of seasons. See Figures 155 and 160.

Next, make posts (*C*) and cut ¼-in.-deep mortise holes into them, and into partitions (*B*) as shown in Figure 160, for the tenons on the ends of the rails, which will be fitted to these holes. Cut the notches into the tops of (*B*) at the front and into the tops of the posts. Rabbet the rear edges of the ends (*A*), where the back (*D*) is to be joined to them.

Locate the places where drawer guides and drawer runs are to be screwed fast to these ends (*A*) and (*B*), and make and fasten them in place at this time. Rabbet the front edges of the posts and glue the posts to the ends (*A*).

Make the rails (*F*) and (*G*). Glue brackets (*H*) to both ends of (*G*). Now assemble the parts which have been made. Make and fasten strips (*K*), (*L*), and (*M*) to the upper parts of the desk. The top is later fastened in place with screws passed through these from below, as shown in Figure 160.

Make and fasten the feet, as shown in Figures 154 and 155.

The quarter columns are made by gluing four strips of wood together, as shown in Figure 161. Once turned, these may easily be split apart without damage, and the two which are to be used will be perfect quarter columns which may be glued into the niches prepared for them.

Two types of construction are shown for the drawers, detailed in Figures 157 and 158. The dovetail joints are preferable if one has the time and skill to make them. Once dovetails have been cut out and properly fitted, the drawer fronts may be raised, as shown. The way this is best done has been described in Chapter 5, and we deem it unnecessary to repeat the instructions here.

Appropriate hardware as shown for this piece of furniture is a type generally used on early eighteenth-century pieces similar in design to this.

### BILL OF MATERIAL

| DESCRIPTION | PIECES | DIMENSIONS |
|---|---|---|
| Ends (A) | 2 | ¾ x 18½ x 29¼ |
| Inside ends of drawer sections (B) | 2 | ¾ x 17¾ x 29¼ |
| Front posts back of quarter columns (C) | 2 | ¾ x 2 x 29¼ |
| Back (D) | 1 | ¾ x 24¾ x 50 |
| Rail under top (E) | 1 | ¾ x 2 x 49 |
| Rails between drawers (F) | 8 | ¾ x 2 x 13½ |
| Rail below middle drawer (G) | 1 | ¾ x 2 x 20½ |
| Small blocks (H) glued to (G) | 2 | 1¼ x 1¼ x 2 |
| Drawer guides (I) | 8 | ¾ x 1½ x 15¾ (See Fig. 160.) |
| Drawer runs (J) | 18 | ¾ x ¾ x 15¾ |
| Strips to fasten top (K) | 2 | ¾ x 1½ x 14¾ |
| Strips to fasten top (L) | 2 | ¾ x 1 x 13¾ |
| Strips to fasten top (M) | 4 | ¾ x ¾ x 14¾ |
| Feet at front of desk (N) | 2 | ¾ x 5 x 16¾ |
| Feet at ends (O) | 4 | ¾ x 5 x 19¼ |
| Feet at rear (P) | 2 | ¾ x 4½ x 15 (See Fig. 154.) |
| Top (Q) | 1 | ¾ x 20 x 52 |
| Quarter columns (R) | 4 | 1 x 1 x 21 (See Fig. 161.) |
| Drawer front (S) | 1 | 15/16 x 3 11/16 x 19 15/16 |
| Drawer fronts (T) | 2 | 15/16 x 3 11/16 x 12 15/16 |
| Drawer fronts (U) | 2 | 15/16 x 4 15/16 x 12 15/16 |
| Drawer fronts (V) | 2 | 15/16 x 5 15/16 x 12 15/16 |
| Drawer fronts (W) | 2 | 15/16 x 6 3/16 x 12 15/16 |
| Drawer sides (X-S) and (X-T) | 6 | ½ x 3 11/16 x 17⅝ |
| Drawer sides (X-U) | 4 | ½ x 4 15/16 x 17⅝ |
| Drawer sides (X-V) | 4 | ½ x 5 15/16 x 17⅝ |
| Drawer sides (X-W) | 4 | ½ x 6 3/16 x 17⅝ |
| Drawer back (Y-S) | 1 | ½ x 3 11/16 x 19 15/16 (Dovetailed back) |
| Drawer backs (Y-T) | 2 | ½ x 3 11/16 x 12 15/16 (Dovetailed back) |
| Drawer backs (Y-U) | 2 | ½ x 4 15/16 x 12 15/16 (Dovetailed back) |
| Drawer backs (Y-V) | 2 | ½ x 5 15/16 x 12 15/16 (Dovetailed back) |
| Drawer backs (Y-W) | 2 | ½ x 6 3/16 x 12 15/16 (Dovetailed back) |
| Drawer bottom (Z-S) (plywood) | 1 | ¼ x 19 5/16 x 17 |
| Drawer bottoms (Z-T) (plywood) | 8 | ¼ x 12 5/16 x 17 |

# 24. Mirror

The mirror shown in Figure 162 may be used with the piece of furniture described in Chapter 23 (Fig. 153) or it may be hung on the wall by itself. Figure 163 shows the proportionate relationship of the two pieces when used together.

The construction presents no great difficulty. Mortise-and-tenon joints are employed to hold the rails and stiles together. For a mirror as large as this, the type of construction employed is desirable because it makes a frame so joined quite sturdy.

A standard-size crown molding is used at the top. The panel is raised as described for the wastebasket in Chapter 5. A beveled-edge mirror may be used. With the raised panel above it, such a mirror would be quite appropriate. The dentils under the crown molding add interest to the design. They may be glued to the frame.

## BILL OF MATERIAL

| DESCRIPTION | PIECES | DIMENSIONS |
|---|---|---|
| Stiles | 2 | ⅞ x 2½ x 38½ |
| Bottom rail | 1 | ⅞ x 3 x 23½ |
| Upper rail | 1 | ⅞ x 4⅝ x 23½ |
| Rail between panel and glass | 1 | ⅞ x 1½ x 23½ |
| Top | 1 | ½ x 3¼ x 29 |
| Panel | 1 | ¾ x 4¾ x 20¼ |
| Filler strip under crown molding | 1 | ⅜ x 2¼ x 24½ |
| Crown molding, standard | | 2⅝ x 36 |
| Dentils | 27 | ¼ x ¾ x 1 |

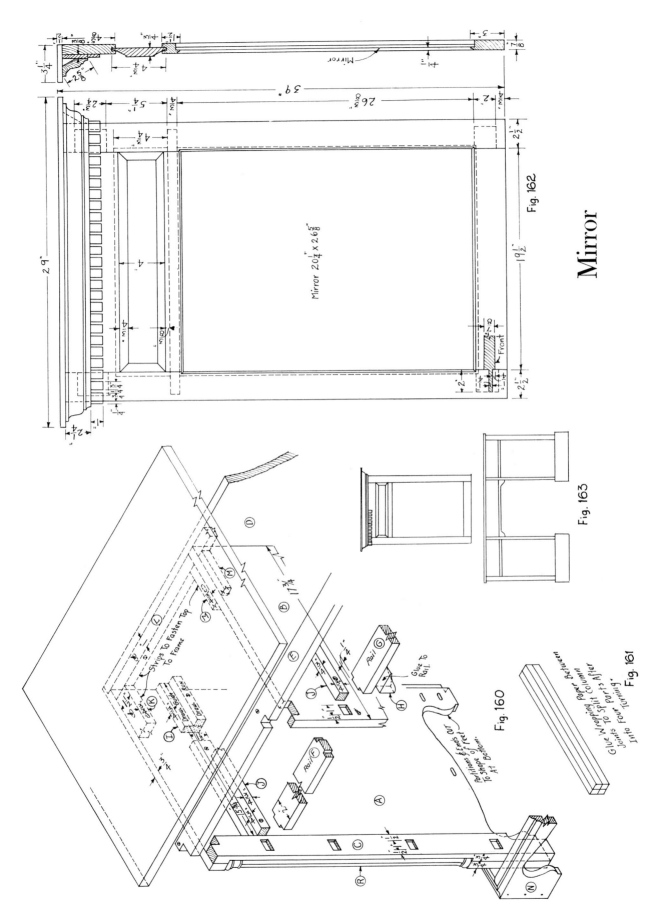

Mirror

Mirror 20¼" × 26⅝"

Fig. 162

Fig. 163

Rail G

Glue To Rail.

Rail F

Portions & Ends cut To Shape of Feet At Bottom.

Fig. 160

Strips To Fasten Top To Frame

Dowel Guide

Glue Wrapping Paper Between To Split Column After Joints Four Turning.

Fig. 161

# 25. Small Desk

Fig. 164

The small desk shown in Figure 164 is ideal for a room in which a minimum of space is available. Its design is, moreover, a fine one for students. The drawers are large enough to hold standard-size stationery, and there is enough knee room for comfort. The design is plain, and of a kind which will look well with other furniture of traditional or contemporary design. The construction is sturdy and comparatively inexpensive.

To make the desk, first glue up ends (A), partition (B), and back (H). Plane and sandpaper these, and then rabbet the back edges of (A).

Get out stock for all frames which separate and support the drawers. Assemble these frames, and sandpaper them smooth. Make the grooves in (A) and (B) to which the frames are fastened. Screw the frames fast to (A) and (B), without using glue. See Figure 167. Fasten the back with 4-penny finish nails. Then cut molding on the upper edges of the base pieces, and fasten these to the desk.

Several types of construction are shown for the drawers in Figures 168, 169, and 170. Although the construction shown in Figure 168 is recommended, you may choose the one which best suits the conditions under which the desk has to be built, taking into consideration such things as the ability of the builder, the type of equipment at hand, and the amount of time available.

The top is fastened last with wood screws. Long slots are drilled through the upper frames for these to allow for seasonal contraction or expansion of the top.

82

## BILL OF MATERIAL

| DESCRIPTION | PIECES | DIMENSIONS |
| --- | --- | --- |
| Ends (A) | 2 | ¾ x 20 x 29¼ |
| Partition between drawers and kneehole (B) | 1 | ¾ x 19¼ x 29¼ |
| Front rails (C) | 5 | ¾ x 2 x 11¼ |
| Rear rails (D) | 5 | ¾ x 2 x 11¼ |
| Long front rails (E) | 2 | ¾ x 2 x 23¾ |
| Long rear rails (F) | 2 | ¾ x 2 x 23¾ |
| Drawer run rails (G) | 14 | ¾ x 2 x 18¼ |
| Back (H) | 1 | ¾ x 25¼ x 36 |
| Base at rear (I) | 1 | ¾ x 5 x 38¼ |
| Base at ends (J) | 4 | ¾ x 5 x 21½ |
| Base at front (K) | 1 | ¾ x 5 x 14 |
| Short base at front (L) | 1 | ¾ x 5 x 2¼ |
| Top (M) | 1 | ¾ x 22½ x 40 |
| Upper drawer front (long) (N) | 1 | ¾ x 3¹⁵⁄₁₆ x 23⁷⁄₁₆ |
| Upper drawer front (short) (O) | 1 | ¾ x 3¹⁵⁄₁₆ x 10¹⁵⁄₁₆ |
| Second drawer front (P) | 1 | ¾ x 4¹⁵⁄₁₆ x 10¹⁵⁄₁₆ |
| Third drawer front (Q) | 1 | ¾ x 4¹⁵⁄₁₆ x 10¹⁵⁄₁₆ |
| Lower drawer front (R) | 1 | ¾ x 6¹⁵⁄₁₆ x 10¹⁵⁄₁₆ |
| Upper drawer sides (S) | 4 | ⅝ x 3¹⁵⁄₁₆ x 19 |
| Second drawer sides (T) | 2 | ⅝ x 4¹⁵⁄₁₆ x 19 |
| Third drawer sides (U) | 2 | ⅝ x 4¹⁵⁄₁₆ x 19 |
| Lower drawer sides (V) | 2 | ⅝ x 6¹⁵⁄₁₆ x 19 |
| Drawer back (long) (W) | 1 | ⅜ x 3⁵⁄₁₆ x 22¹³⁄₁₆ |
| Drawer back, upper drawer (X) | 1 | ⅜ x 3⁵⁄₁₆ x 10⁵⁄₁₆ |
| Drawer backs, second and third drawers (Y) | 2 | ⅜ x 4⁵⁄₁₆ x 10⁵⁄₁₆ |
| Drawer back, lower drawer (Z) | 1 | ⅜ x 6⁵⁄₁₆ x 10⁵⁄₁₆ |
| Drawer bottom, long drawer (plywood) (A-A) | 1 | ¼ x 18¾ x 22¹³⁄₁₆ |
| Drawer bottoms, small drawers (plywood) (B-B) | 4 | ¼ x 10⁵⁄₁₆ x 18¾ |

# Small Desk

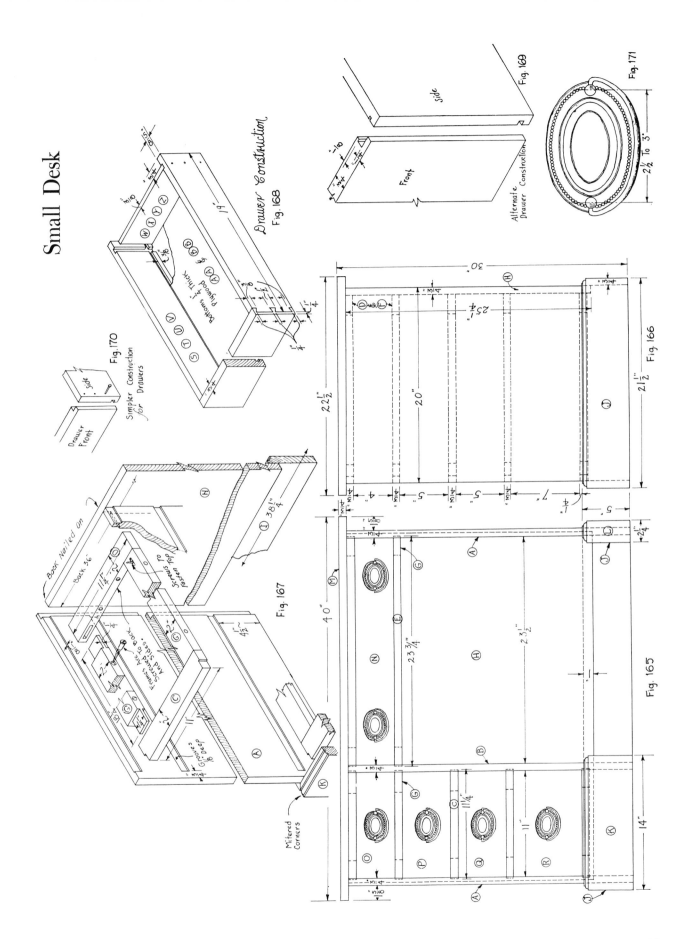

Drawer Construction
Fig. 168

Side

Front

Fig. 169

Alternate Drawer Construction

2½ To 3"

Fig. 171

Bottoms ⅜" Thick plywood

Fig. 170

Simpler Construction for Drawers

Side

Drawer Front

Back Nailed On

Back 36"

Screws To fasten Top

Frames Are Screwed To Back And Sides.

Mitered Corners

Fig. 167

Fig. 166

Fig. 165

## 26. Small Dresser

Fig. 172

# Small Dresser

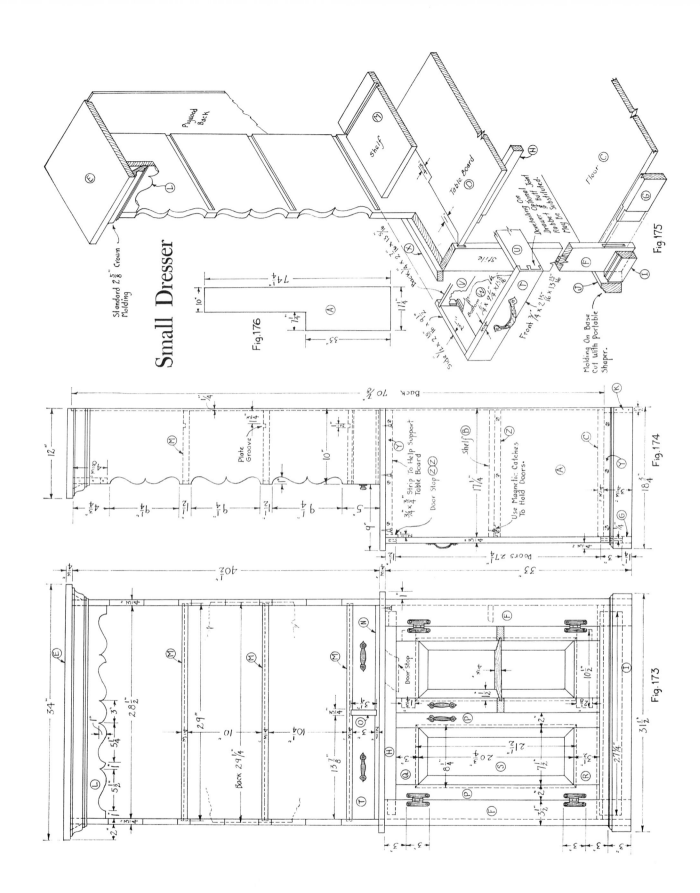

Standard 2⅝" Crown Molding

Plywood Back

Fig.176

Fig.175

Fig.174

Fig.173

85

The lovely little piece of furniture shown in Figure 172 may be used for a number of purposes. A few of them are suggested by examining the photograph. It makes a nice china cabinet, or it could serve as a bookcase. A fine collection of one kind or another could be shown off to good advantage on its upper shelves.

For so handsome a piece, it is comparatively easy to build; and the builder should have a feeling of justifiable pride in its ownership.

First, glue up the ends, as shown in Figure 176. Plane and sandpaper them to a good smooth finish, and then rabbet the back edges. Next, lay out and cut the grooves to which the shelves will be joined. This may be done with the dado-head on the circular saw, with an overhead arbor saw, with an electric hand router, or with an ordinary router plane. Since the grooves are stopped ½ in. from the front edge, this part of the groove will have to be finished with a chisel. Next, lay out and saw the shaped front edges, on the ends, as shown in Figures 174 and 175. Smooth these with a file and sandpaper.

Glue up the wide shelf (B), bottom (C), and table-board. Make partition (O). Run the plate grooves along the back of one side of the upper shelves. The pieces you have made may now be assembled. To do this, screw strips (Y) and (Z) to the insides of the ends, first drilling screw holes in both directions. Then glue partition (O) to shelf (M) and (N). The grain on this partition should, of course, run vertically. Glue the upper shelves to the grooves in the ends. Then screw fast the bottom, the wide shelf, and the table-board. Also make and attach strips (X), as shown in Figure 175.

Make the frame consisting of stiles (F) and rails (H) and (G). Nail this frame to the front with 4-penny finishing nails. Make and fasten the base.

Make canopy (L), and nail it fast to the ends. Then fit the crown molding in place, and put on the top (E). Be sure to cut a rabbet along the back edge of the top before nailing it fast to the ends.

Cut the plywood back, and nail it fast to the ends, shelves, bottom, and top.

Make the paneled doors. See Chapter 5 for instructions on raising the panels. Fit and fasten the doors.

Make the drawers, and fit them to the openings between the two lower shelves in the upper section. Putting on door and drawer handles finishes the job.

## BILL OF MATERIAL

| DESCRIPTION | PIECES | DIMENSIONS |
|---|---|---|
| Ends (A) | 2 | ¾ x 10 x 74¼ |
| | 2 | ¾ x 7¼ x 33 |
| Shelf (B) | 1 | ¾ x 17 x 28½ |
| Bottom (C) | 1 | ¾ x 17 x 28½ |
| Table-board (D) | 1 | ¾ x 18¾ x 32 |
| Top (E) | 1 | ¾ x 12 x 34 |
| Stiles (F) | 2 | ¾ x 3½ x 33 |
| Bottom rail (G) | 1 | ¾ x 3 x 27¼ |
| Rail above doors (H) | 1 | ¾ x 1½ x 27¼ |
| Front base (I) | 1 | ¾ x 3 x 31½ |
| End base (J) | 1 | ¾ x 3 x 18¾ |
| Base at rear (K) | 1 | ½ x 4¼ x 28½ |
| Canopy board (L) | 1 | ¾ x 4⅜ x 28½ |
| Shelves (M) | 3 | ¾ x 9¾ x 29 |
| Shelf under drawers (N) | 1 | ½ x 9¾ x 28½ |
| Partition between drawers (O) | 1 | ¾ x 9¾ x 3¼ |
| Door stiles (P) | 4 | ¾ x 2 x 27¼ |
| Upper door rails (Q) | 2 | ¾ x 3 x 10½ |
| Lower door rails (R) | 2 | ¾ x 3½ x 10½ |
| Door panels (S) | 2 | ¾ x 8¼ x 21½ |
| Drawer fronts (T) | 2 | ¾ x 2¹⁵⁄₁₆ x 13¹³⁄₁₆ |
| Drawer sides (U) | 4 | ½ x 2¹⁵⁄₁₆ x 9½ |
| Drawer backs (V) | 2 | ¼ x 2⁷⁄₁₆ x 13⁵⁄₁₆ |
| Drawer bottoms (plywood) (W) | 2 | ¼ x 9¼ x 13⁵⁄₁₆ |
| Strips at end of table-board (X) | 2 | ¾ x 1 x 19 |
| Strips under table-board and bottom, in lower part of dresser (Y) | 4 | ¾ x ¾ x 16½ |
| Strips under shelf in lower part of dresser (Z) | 2 | ¾ x ¾ x 17 |
| Door stop (Z-Z) | 1 | ½ x 1¾ x 28½ |
| Crown molding, Standard | | 2⅝ x 60 |

Fig. 177

Much of the appeal of the rather handsome cabinet bookcase shown in Figure 177 comes from its simple lines, its good proportions, and from the beauty of the wood grain. Poplar, of which this piece is made, is a handsomely grained wood, and when the figure of the grain is not obscured by the finish, the effect is indeed charming.

The joint at the top is dovetailed, as shown in Figure 179. This type of construction enhances the beauty and value of a piece of furniture such

# Cabinet Bookcase

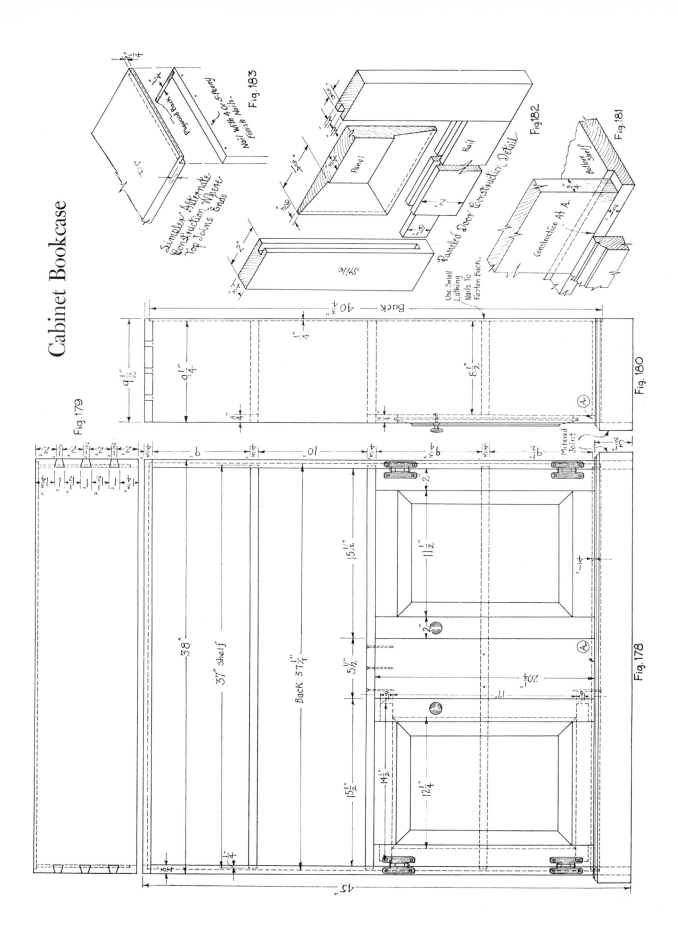

Fig. 183

Fig. 179

Fig. 180

Fig. 178

Fig. 181

Fig. 182

Simpler Alternate Construction Where Top Joins Ends

Paneled Door Construction Detail

Construction At A

Use Small Lathing Nails To Fasten Back.

Nail with 4 or 5-penny finish nails.

Plywood Back

Panel

Rail

Stile

Bottom Shelf

Mitered Joint

as this, if time and necessary skill are employed to good advantage. However, for those wishing to simplify the construction, they may use the method shown in Figure 183.

Little further need be said about how to build so simple a piece of furniture as this, except to urge a careful perusal of details given in the drawings, Figures 178 to 183. The method of raising panels and constructing doors of this type has been described in earlier chapters, especially in Chapter 5.

Magnetic door catches should be used under the shelf to hold the doors shut.

## BILL OF MATERIAL

| DESCRIPTION | PIECES | DIMENSIONS |
| --- | --- | --- |
| Ends | 2 | ¾ x 9½ x 45 |
| Top | 1 | ¾ x 9½ x 38 |
| Two upper shelves | 2 | ¾ x 9¼ x 37 |
| Lower shelf (behind doors) | 1 | ¾ x 8½ x 37 |
| Floor | 1 | ¾ x 9¼ x 37 |
| Stile between doors | 1 | ¾ x 5½ x 20¼ |
| Front of base | 1 | ¾ x 3½ x 39½ |
| Ends of base | 2 | ¾ x 3½ x 10¼ |
| Door stiles | 4 | ¾ x 2 x 20¼ |
| Door rails | 4 | ¾ x 2 x 14½ |
| Door panels | 2 | ¾ x 12¼ x 17 |
| Back (plywood) | 1 | ¼ x 37¼ x 40¾ |

# 28.  Breakfront Bookcase

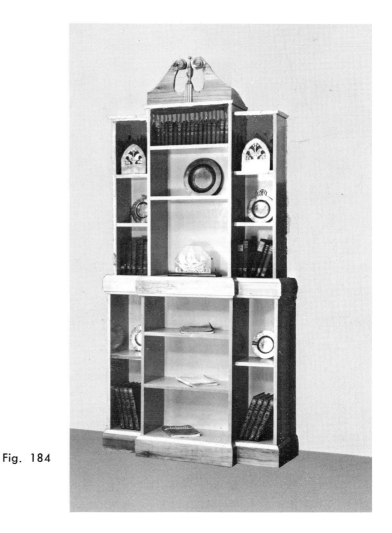

Fig. 184

The breakfront bookcase is a bit different from most bookcases in that it has areas, especially in the lower section, for books which do not fit into an ordinary bookcase. It can provide space for an attractive flower arrangement or some other special display such as one might want to make around Christmastime. As Figure 184 shows, this bookcase, besides its beauty and its imposing height, has great versatility.

A great deal of its charm is derived from the interesting manner of dividing its various areas, and from having the front in two different planes. The breakfront idea, with its two minor flanking areas receding from the dominant central area adds considerable interest to this design. It has many other features which make it attractive, such as the well-shaped hand-carved, swan-necked pediment. One does not readily grow tired of looking at so distinctive a piece of furniture.

Despite this piece's versatility, its construction is quite simple. To build it, first cut out, plane, and sand the four ends shown in Figures 188 and 189. Next, make the table-boards, and shelves. Rabbet the back edges of the ends (Fig. 189) so the back may be nailed on and not have its edges showing. On all four ends lay out lines where

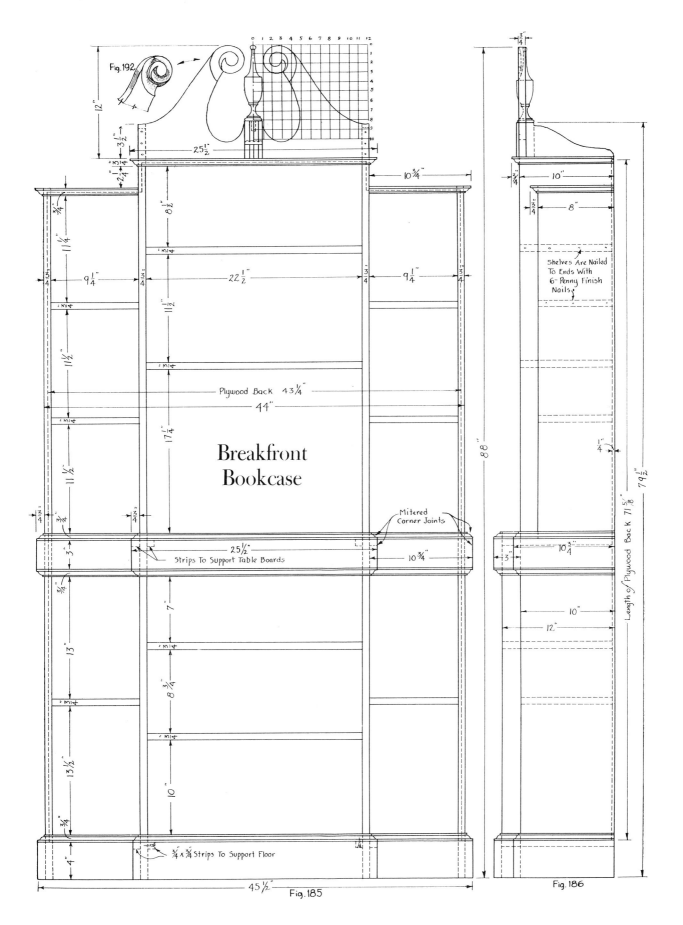

Fig. 192

Breakfront
Bookcase

Plywood Back 43¼"
44"

Mitered
Corner Joints

Strips To Support Table Boards

¾" x ¾" Strips To Support Floor

25½"

10¾"

9¼"

45½"

Fig. 185

8'8"

Shelves Are Nailed
To Ends With
6-Penny Finish
Nails

Length of Plywood Back 71⅝"

79½"

Fig. 186

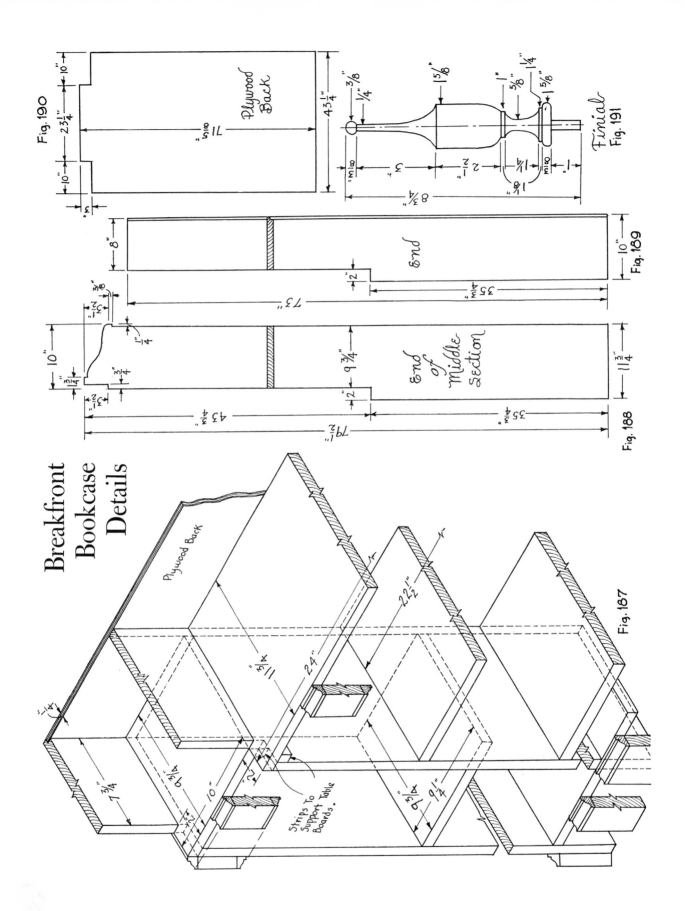

Breakfront Bookcase Details

Fig. 190

Plywood Back

Finial
Fig. 191

Fig. 189

End

End of Middle Section

Fig. 188

Plywood Back

Strips To Support Table Boards.

Fig. 187

shelves are to be fastened to them. Since all table-boards are level with each other, and all floorboards are also level with each other, strips must be screwed fast to the ends of the middle section (Fig. 188) to support them where they meet on both sides of the ends, since it would be very difficult to nail all of them fast at these places. Wood screws may then be used here in place of nails to fasten all of these members together securely. Six-penny finishing nails may be used at other places to nail shelves, floorboards, and table-boards, such as to the ends, for example.

The pieces which go to make up the apron running around the middle of the bookcase, are joined with miter joints, as shown in Figure 187. This is also true of the base, and of the molding applied at these two places, and around the top of the bookcase. It is possible, of course, to make the apron boards 1½ in. wider than shown in the bill of material, and cut molding on both edges on a shaper instead of adding it to both edges as shown here. The same thing can be done when making the base. Inexpensive molding may always be purchased, however, and using it is the simplest way of doing the job.

Figure 192 shows how to carve the scrolls on the swan-necked pediment. The carving which needs to be done here is not difficult, and adds much to the beauty of the bookcase.

## BILL OF MATERIAL

| DESCRIPTION | PIECES | DIMENSIONS |
|---|---|---|
| Ends | 2 | ¾ x 10 x 73 |
| Ends of middle section | 2 | ¾ x 11¾ x 79½ |
| Table-board, middle section | 1 | ¾ x 11¾ x 24 |
| Table-boards, end section | 2 | ¾ x 9¾ x 10 |
| Shelves and floorboard, lower middle section | 3 | ¾ x 11¾ x 22½ |
| Shelves and floorboards, lower end sections | 4 | ¾ x 9¾ x 9¼ |
| Shelves, middle upper section | 2 | ¾ x 9¾ x 22½ |
| Shelves, upper end sections | 4 | ¾ x 7¾ x 9¼ |
| Tops, upper end sections | 2 | ¾ x 8 x 9¼ |
| Top, upper middle section | 1 | ¾ x 10 x 22½ |
| Swan-necked pediment | 1 | ¾ x 12 x 24 |
| Molding strip under finial | 1 | ¼ x 1¾ x 3⅞ |
| Block under finial back of pediment | 1 | ¾ x 1¾ x 3⅞ |
| Aprons at ends | 2 | ¾ x 3 x 10¾ |
| Front aprons, end sections | 2 | ¾ x 3 x 10¾ |
| Short pieces on apron | 2 | ¾ x 3 x 3 |
| Long apron, middle section | 1 | ¾ x 3 x 25½ |
| Base on ends | 2 | ¾ x 4 x 10¾ |
| Front base, end sections | 2 | ¾ x 4 x 10¾ |
| Short pieces on base | 2 | ¾ x 4 x 3 |
| Long base, front of middle section | 1 | ¾ x 4 x 25½ |
| Strips to support floor of middle section | 2 | ¾ x ¾ x 11¾ |
| Strips to support floor, end sections | 2 | ¾ x ¾ x 9¾ |
| Strips to support table-board, middle section | 2 | ¾ x ¾ x 11¾ |
| Strips to support table-boards, end sections | 2 | ¾ x ¾ x 9¾ |
| Finial | 1 | 1⅝ diam. x 8¾ |
| Back (plywood) | 1 | ¼ x 43¼ x 71⅝ |

Molding — 23 ft. 8 in. total. A bit more will be needed to allow for waste in sawing and fitting miters.

# 29. Paneled Magazine and Coffee Table

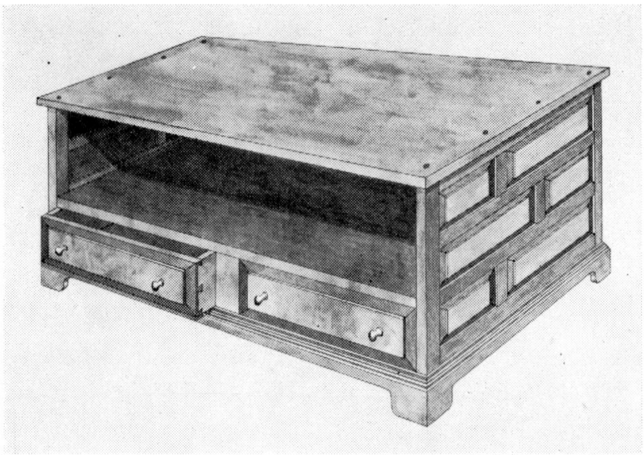

Fig. 193

Figure 193 shows a useful and somewhat different kind of coffee table. It has a large magazine storage area above its two drawers, and one which keeps the magazines flat yet easily accessible, since it is open on both sides. Storing the magazines beneath leaves the top free for other suitable purposes. Moreover, the generous drawer storage space is still another good utilitarian feature.

The handsomely paneled ends, back, and drawer fronts give this small and useful piece of furniture an air of distinction not often found in a coffee table.

Make the paneled ends and back first. Rails and stiles are grooved for the raised panels. To raise panels like this, refer to Chapter 5. The ends of the table are notched out on the bottoms at the back, so the face of the frame of the paneled back will be flush with the back edges of the ends, as shown at the lower right in Figure 195.

Drawers have dovetail construction, as shown in Figures 193 and 197. The shelf and the frame holding up the drawers are secured fast with finishing nails.

The top is screwed fast to both ends. The heads of the screws are sunk ¼ in. below the surface and are then capped with wooden plugs, planed and sanded down even with the surface. These add a touch of decoration to an otherwise plain top.

The footed base is put together at the corners with nailed and glued miter joints.

**BILL OF MATERIAL**

| DESCRIPTION | PIECES | DIMENSIONS |
|---|---|---|
| Corner stiles in ends | 4 | ¾ x 1¼ x 16 |
| Short stiles in ends | 6 | ¾ x 1¼ x 3¾ |
| Three upper rails in ends | 6 | ¾ x 1¼ x 17½ |
| Bottom rails in ends | 2 | ¾ x 2½ x 17½ |
| Panels in ends | 6 | ⅝ x 3¾ x 9½ |
| Panels in ends | 6 | ⅝ x 3¾ x 6¼ |
| Short stile between drawers | 1 | ¾ x 3 x 4¾ (See Fig. 194.) |
| Long rails in frame under drawers | 2 | ¾ x 2 x 37 (See Fig. 199.) |
| End rails in frame under drawers | 2 | ¾ x 2 x 16¼ (See Fig. 199.) |
| Middle rail in frame under drawers | 1 | ¾ x 4½ x 16¼ (See Fig. 199.) |
| Drawer guide in frame under drawers | 1 | ¾ x 3 x 15½ (See Fig. 199.) |
| Upper rail in frame back of drawers | 1 | ¾ x 1¼ x 38½ |
| Lower rail in frame back of drawers | 1 | ¾ x 2½ x 38½ |
| Stiles in frame back of drawers | 5 | ¾ x 1¼ x 3¾ |
| Panels in frame back of drawers | 2 | ⅝ x 3¾ x 10 |
| Panels in frame back of drawers | 2 | ⅝ x 3¾ x 7⅛ |
| Shelf above drawers | 1 | ¾ x 17¾ x 37 |
| Top | 1 | ¾ x 20 x 40 |
| Base | 2 | ¾ x 2½ x 40 |
| Base | 2 | ¾ x 2½ x 20 |
| Drawer fronts | 2 | ⅞ x 4¹¹⁄₁₆ x 16¹⁵⁄₁₆ |
| Drawer sides | 4 | ½ x 4¹¹⁄₁₆ x 17⅝ |
| Drawer backs | 2 | ½ x 4¹¹⁄₁₆ x 16¹⁵⁄₁₆ |
| Drawer bottoms (plywood) | 2 | ¼ x 16⁷⁄₁₆ x 17⅛ |
| Drawer pulls | 4 | ⅞ x 2⅛ |

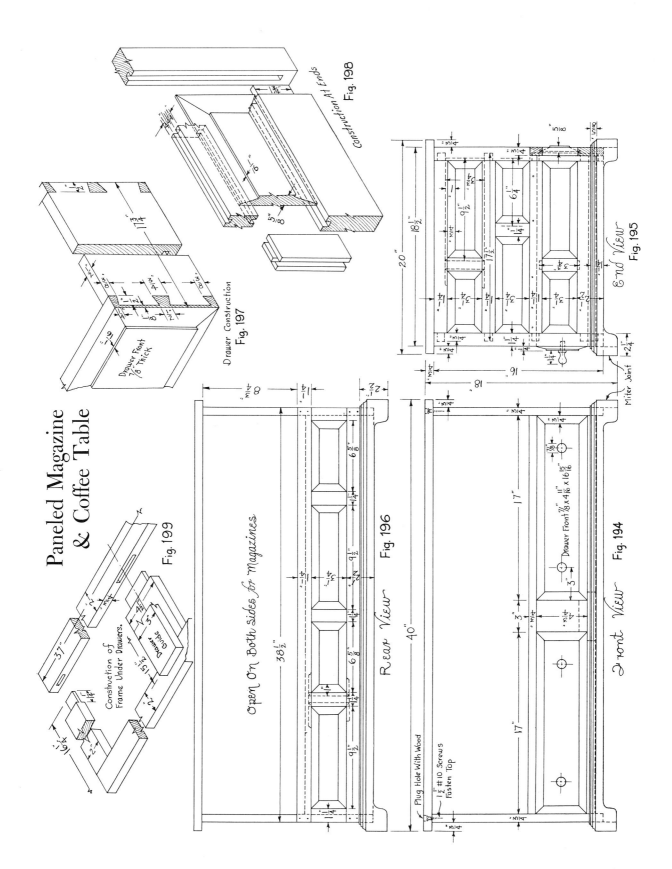

Paneled Magazine & Coffee Table

Fig. 198 — Construction At Ends

Fig. 197 — Drawer Construction

Drawer Front 7/8" Thick

Fig. 199 — Construction of Frame Under Drawers.

Drawer Guide

Fig. 195 — End View

Miter Joint

Fig. 196 — Rear View

Open On Both Sides for Magazines

Fig. 194 — Front View

Drawer Front 7/8" x 4 1/16" x 16 5/16"

Plug Hole With Wood

1 1/2" #10 Screws Fasten Top

# 30. Dutch Cupboard

Fig. 200

Many collectors in Eastern Pennsylvania, and the surrounding area, take great pride in the ownership of large roomy Dutch cupboards, similar to the one shown in Figure 200. The author owns one slightly larger than the one we show here. Such a cupboard is capable of holding, protecting, and showing off to great advantage, fine collections of china, pewter, silverware, bric-a-brac, or what have you, behind the glass doors of the upper part. In addition to this, it has two large cupboards, and six large drawers in the bottom section, in which a great number of things may be stored. The space below the upper doors is capable of holding long rows of books, and has room to spare for displaying other items.

The difficulties in building a cupboard like this are not great and the pride of ownership, if one has the room for one, is worth the trouble.

Start by gluing up two ends (A), a partition (B), and two partitions (B-1), as shown in Figures 202 and 203. Rabbet the ends to receive the plywood back (N-N).

Shelves (L) and floors (K) are made next. Strips are cut for drawer guides and drawer runs,

# Dutch Cupboard

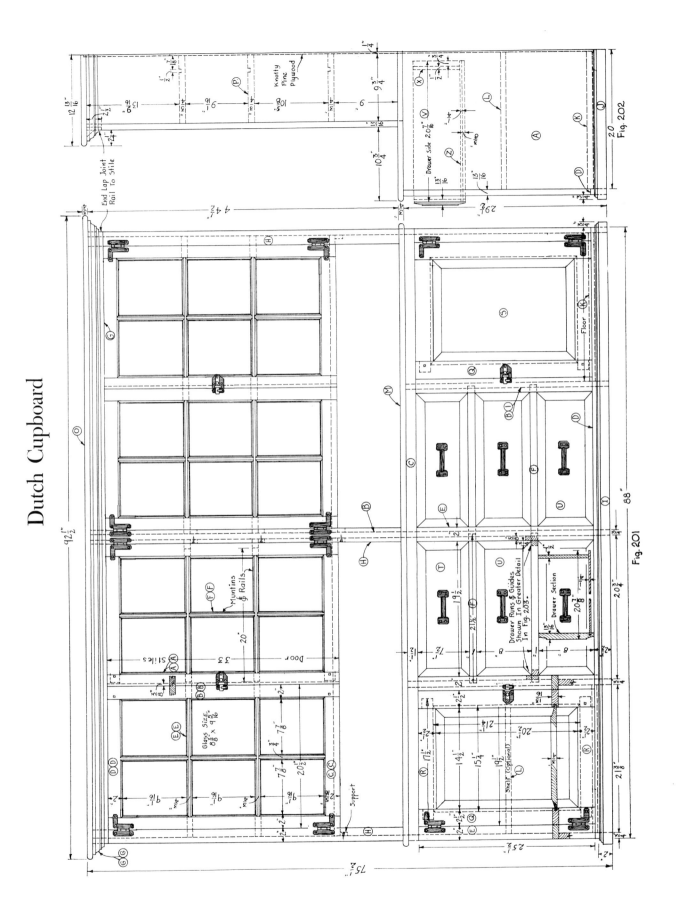

Fig. 202

Fig. 201

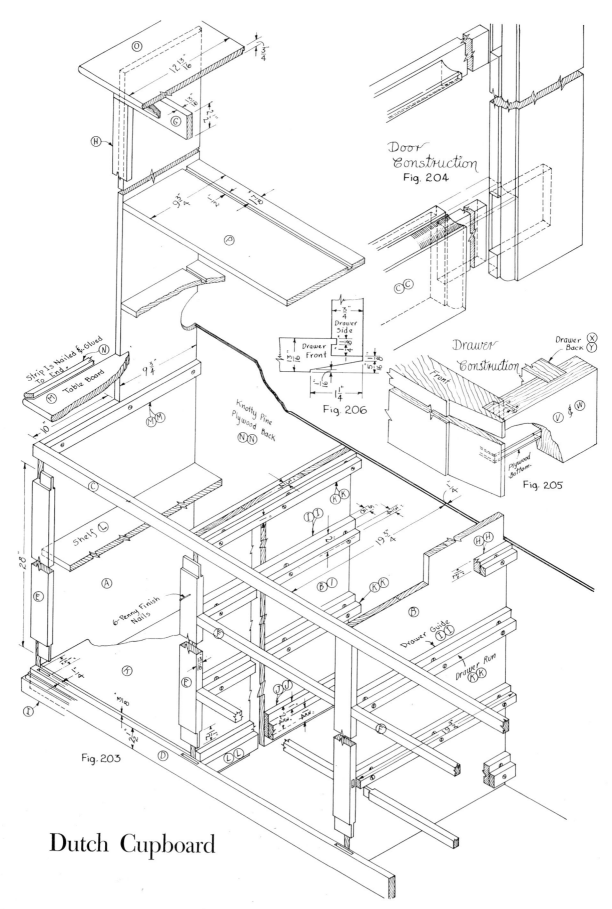

Door Construction
Fig. 204

Drawer Construction

Fig. 205

Fig. 206

Drawer Side

Drawer Front

Strip Is Nailed & Glued To End.

Table Board

Knotty Pine Plywood Back

Shelf

6-Penny Finish Nails

Drawer Guide

Drawer Run

Fig. 203

Plywood Bottom.

Dutch Cupboard

## BILL OF MATERIAL

| DESCRIPTION | PIECES | DIMENSIONS |
|---|---|---|
| Ends (A) | 2 | ¾ x 10 x 74¾ |
| | 2 | ¾ x 10 x 29½ |
| Partition (B) | 1 | ¾ x 9¾ x 74¾ |
| | 1 | ¾ x 10 x 29½ |
| Partitions (B-1) | 2 | ¾ x 19¾ x 29½ |
| Rail above paneled doors (C) | 1 | 13/16 x 1½ x 88 |
| Rail below paneled doors (D) | 1 | 13/16 x 2½ x 88 |
| Stiles in lower frame (E) | 5 | 13/16 x 2 x 28 (See Fig. 203.) |
| Rails between drawers (F) | 4 | 13/16 x 1 x 21½ |
| Long rail under crown molding (G) | 1 | 13/16 x 2½ x 88 |
| Stiles in upper section (H) | 3 | 13/16 x 2 x 44½ |
| Base front (I) | 1 | ¾ x 2 x 89½ |
| Base ends (J) | 2 | ¾ x 2 x 21 9/16 |
| Floorboards (K) | 2 | ¾ x 19¾ x 21⅜ |
| Shelf boards (L) | 2 | ¾ x 19¾ x 21⅜ |
| Table-board (M) | 1 | ¾ x 21 5/16 x 89½ |
| Strips at ends of table-board (N) | 2 | ¾ x ¾ x 21 9/16 |
| Top (O) | 1 | ¾ x 12 13/16 x 92½ |
| Shelves in upper section (P) | 6 | ¾ x 9¾ x 42⅞ |
| Stiles, lower doors (Q) | 4 | 13/16 x 2½ x 25½ |
| Rails, lower doors (R) | 4 | 13/16 x 2½ x 17½ |
| Panels, lower doors (S) | 2 | ¾ x 15¼ x 21¼ |
| Upper drawer fronts (T) | 2 | 13/16 x 7 7/16 x 19 7/16 |
| Middle and lower drawer fronts (U) | 4 | 13/16 x 7 15/16 x 19 7/16 |
| Upper drawer sides (V) | 4 | ¾ x 7 7/16 x 20 7/16 |
| Middle and lower drawer sides (W) | 8 | ¾ x 7 15/16 x 20 7/16 |
| Upper drawer backs (X) | 2 | ½ x 6 13/16 x 18 15/16 |
| Middle and lower drawer backs (Y) | 4 | ½ x 7 5/16 x 18 15/16 |
| Drawer bottoms (plywood) (Z) | 6 | ¼ x 18 15/16 x 20 7/16 |
| Upper door stiles (A-A) | 6 | 13/16 x 2 x 33 |
| Upper door stiles (B-B) | 2 | 13/16 x 2⅜ x 33 |
| Lower rails on upper door (C-C) | 4 | 13/16 x 2 5/16 x 20 |
| Upper rails on upper doors (D-D) | 4 | 13/16 x 2 x 20 |
| Narrow rail on upper doors (E-E) | 8 | 13/16 x ¾ x 20 |
| Muntins (F-F) | 12 | 13/16 x ¾ x 9 9/16 |
| Crown molding (G-G) | 12 ft. of 2⅝ standard molding (approx.) |  |
| Strips under table-board (H-H) | 4 | ⅝ x 1½ x 19¾ |
| Drawer guide strips (I-I) | 8 | ⅝ x 2 x 19¾ |
| Lower drawer guide strips (J-J) | 4 | ⅝ x 2¾ x 19¾ |
| Drawer run strips (K-K) | 12 | ¾ x 1 x 19¾ |
| Lower drawer run strips (L-L) | 4 | ¾ x 1¾ x 19¾ |
| Strips under table-board (M-M) | 2 | ¾ x 1 x 19¾ |
| Backs (plywood) (N-N) | 2 | 43⅝ x 72¾ |

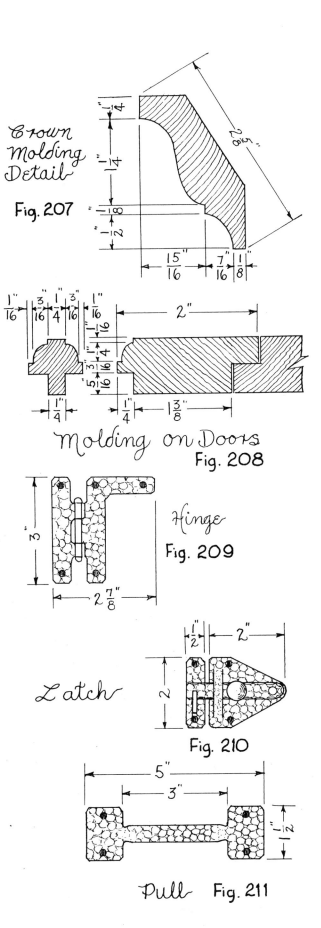

Crown Molding Detail
Fig. 207

Molding on Doors
Fig. 208

Hinge
Fig. 209

Latch
Fig. 210

Pull Fig. 211

and these are screwed fast to the partitions. Strips ¾ in. thick by 2⅛ in. wide may be screwed fast to the ends under floorboards (K) to help support the floorboards, though these are not absolutely necessary, and are, therefore, not shown in our drawings.

All is now in readiness to assemble the pieces we have enumerated above. Six-penny finishing nails are used to nail shelves and floorboards to ends and partitions. Guide strips (J-J) and drawer runs (L-L) should be screwed fast after the floor boards have been nailed to the (B-1) partitions, though these same pieces, which are to be fastened to the lower end of partition (B), may be screwed fast before the back is nailed to it. As a matter of fact, it is best to do it this way.

The frame which goes on the front, at the bottom, should now be made and nailed fast. Figure 203 shows how it is put together with mortise-and-tenon joints.

Make and fasten the table-board next. Then make the upper shelves, and nail them to the ends and middle partition. Make the frame to go on the front of the upper section, and nail it fast. Then make and fasten the top (O).

Now put on the crown molding and the base. These are mitered at the corners where they join, as shown in Figures 201, 202, and 203.

Paneled doors, like those shown on the lower part, should be made as described in Chapter 5. When making the drawers, refer to the construc-

tion details given in Figures 205 and 206. Other details for making these will be found in Figures 201 and 202.

The most difficult parts to make are the glazed doors which enclose the shelves in the upper section. Unless the right kind of equipment for making these is available, we advise ordering them from a planing mill which has this equipment and can make them at nominal cost. For those who own equipment to shape the moldings required, and have the necessary skill to do the work, the making of such doors is no drawback. Construction details for the doors are shown in Figure 204. Muntins, or mullions, as they are more commonly called, are coped at the ends to fit around the molded front part of the rail, just as the ends of the rail are coped to fit the molded part of the stiles. See Figure 204. The rabbeted part of these muntins which holds the glass is as long as the longest part shown at (F-F) in Figure 201. Nothing more than a drop or two of glue is needed to hold these in place where they are joined to the rails, and sometimes even the glue is dispensed with, since they will stay in place without it, once the glass has been installed in the openings, if the joints have been properly fitted. See detail of molding shapes in Figure 208.

Wrought-iron hardware of the type shown in Figures 209, 210, and 211, adds a pleasing finishing touch to this, the largest piece of furniture in this book.

100

# 31. Built-In Cupboard for Difficult-to-Use Corner

Fig. 212                                  Fig. 213

A built-in piece of furniture, such as the cupboard shown in Figures 212 and 213, must, of course, fit the particular corner in which it is to be placed. The height, width, and depth of such a piece must therefore be adapted to the dimensions of the corner for which it is intended. The dimensions given here for this piece cannot of course be strictly adhered to.

Built-in pieces such as this fill a real need in many homes, and it is a worthwhile endeavor to adapt sizes to the particular corner where such a piece of furniture is needed. The corner in the

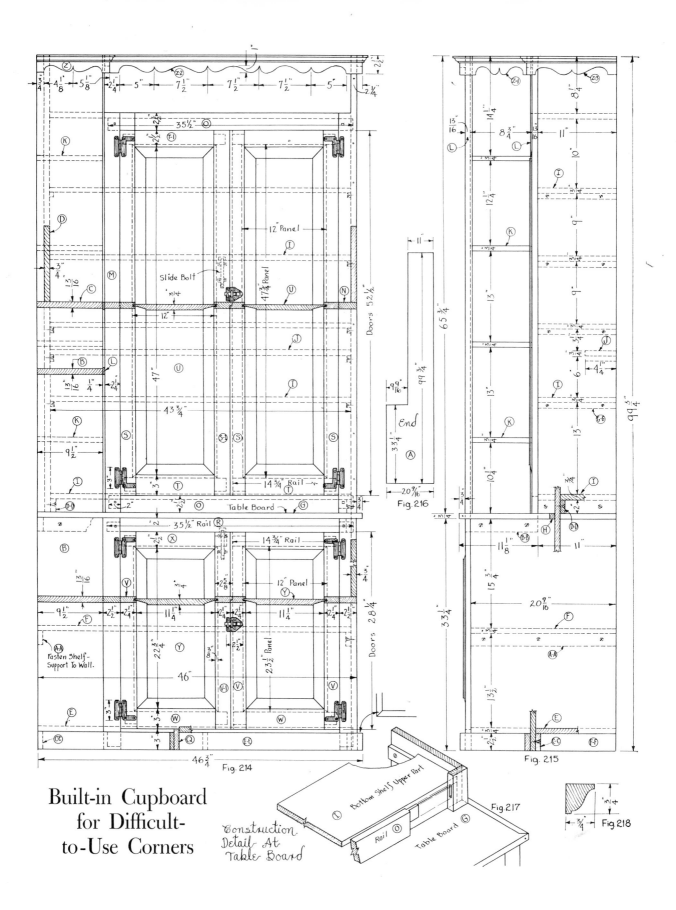

Fig. 214

Fig. 215

Fig. 216

Fig. 217

Fig. 218

Construction
Detail At
Table Board

Bottom Shelf Upper Part

Rail O

Table Board G

Built-in Cupboard
for Difficult-
to-Use Corners

Fig. 219

## BILL OF MATERIAL

| DESCRIPTION | PIECES | DIMENSIONS |
|---|---|---|
| * End (A) | 1 | ¾ x 11 x 99¾ |
| | 1 | ¾ x 9⁹⁄₁₆ x 33¼ |
| End (B) | 1 | ¹³⁄₁₆ x 9½ x 99¾ |
| Partition (C) | 1 | ¹³⁄₁₆ x 9½ x 65¾ |
| Left end, inside of cupboard (upper part) (D) | 1 | ¾ x 11 x 65¾ |
| Floor (lower part) (E) | 1 | ¾ x 20⁹⁄₁₆ x 45¼ |
| Shelf (lower part) (F) | 1 | ¾ x 20⁹⁄₁₆ x 45¼ |
| Table-board (G) | 1 | ¾ x 11⅛ x 46¾ |
| End strip on table-board (H) | 1 | ¾ x ¾ x 22⅛ |
| Shelves (upper part) (I) | 7 | ¾ x 11 x 43¾ |
| Narrow shelf for teacups (J) | 1 | ¾ x 4¼ x 43¾ |
| Shelves for end section (upper part) (K) | 4 | ¾ x 9½ x 8¾ |
| Facing strips, end section (upper part) (L) | 2 | ¼ x ¹³⁄₁₆ x 65¾ |
| Stile, frame of upper part, left end (M) | 1 | ¹³⁄₁₆ x 2¼ x 57½ |
| Stile, frame of upper part, right end (N) | 1 | ¹³⁄₁₆ x 2½ x 65¾ |
| Rails, frame of upper part (O) | 2 | ¹³⁄₁₆ x 2½ x 35½ |
| Stiles, frame of lower part (P) | 2 | ¹³⁄₁₆ x 2½ x 33¼ |
| Bottom rail, frame of lower part (Q) | 1 | ¹³⁄₁₆ x 3 x 35½ |
| Top rail, frame of lower part (R) | 1 | ¹³⁄₁₆ x 2 x 35½ |
| Stiles upper doors (S) | 3 | ¹³⁄₁₆ x 2¼ x 52½ |
| Stile upper doors (S-1) | 1 | ¹³⁄₁₆ x 2⅝ x 52½ |
| Bottom rails, upper doors (T) | 2 | ¹³⁄₁₆ x 3 x 14⅜ |
| Top rails, upper doors (T-1) | 2 | ¹³⁄₁₆ x 2½ x 14¾ |
| Panels, upper doors (U) | 2 | ¾ x 12 x 47¾ |
| Stiles, lower doors (V) | 3 | ¹³⁄₁₆ x 2¼ x 28¼ |
| Stile, lower doors (V-1) | 1 | ¹³⁄₁₆ x 2⅝ x 28¼ |
| Bottom rails, lower doors (W) | 2 | ¹³⁄₁₆ x 3 x 14¾ |
| Top rails, lower doors (X) | 2 | ¹³⁄₁₆ x 2½ x 14¾ |
| Panels, lower doors (Y) | 2 | ¾ x 12 x 23½ |
| Canopy (Z) | 1 | ¾ x 2½ x 10 |
| Canopy (Z-1) | 1 | ¾ x 2½ x 10⁵⁄₁₆ |
| Canopy (Z-2) | 1 | ¾ x 2½ x 37 |
| Canopy (Z-3) | 1 | ¾ x 2½ x 12⁹⁄₁₆ |
| Molding around top, about 6 feet. See Figure 218 | | |
| Shelf supports (A-A) | 2 | ¾ x 2 x 20⁹⁄₁₆ |
| Shelf supports (B-B) | 2 | ¾ x 2 x 9⁹⁄₁₆ |
| Shelf supports (C-C) | 2 | ¾ x 2½ x 20⁹⁄₁₆ |
| Shelf supports (D-D) | 2 | ¾ x 2 x 11 |
| Base (E-E) | 1 | ¾ x 2½ x 46¾ |
| Base (F-F) | 1 | ¾ x 2½ x 22⅛ |
| Shelf supports (G-G) | 8 | ½ x ¾ x 11 |

* Sizes of all pieces may be adjusted to fit the corner of a particular room. Those given are for this particular piece of furniture.

author's home (Figs. 212 and 213) was at one time wasted space. It represented a small area between two doors which are in constant use. The room in which it was built is of medium size, and it was felt that all waste space should be utilized. Moreover, two unsightly water pipes in this corner, added long after the house had been built, cried out to be hidden. The room, which now serves as a dining room, was used as a living room before the new one, shown in the frontispiece, was added to the house; and the first piece of furniture built into this corner was the bookcase shown in Figure 219. Later when the room became a dining area, the bookshelves were redesigned and transformed into this handsome and useful corner cupboard. The cupboard is built of white pine, some of it knotty, but with doors and facing material of a grade free of knots.

The boxing in of the pipes, which is clearly evident in the photographs, does not appear in our working drawings (Figs. 214 and 215) since this is something which may not be necessary in a reproduction.

Figure 213 does not show the molding against the ceiling around the canopy boards. The molding which appears in Figure 212 has been dubbed in by retouching the photograph, since this is an improvement which the author feels should be made.

Since the construction of a number of other pieces of similar furniture has already been described in earlier chapters, a lengthy description of how to go about building this one is omitted. It is assumed that whoever builds a similar piece will have the necessary skills and know-how, and that he will find the photographs and drawings (Figs. 214 to 218), together with the descriptions and directions given in previous chapters, sufficient to guide him in the project.

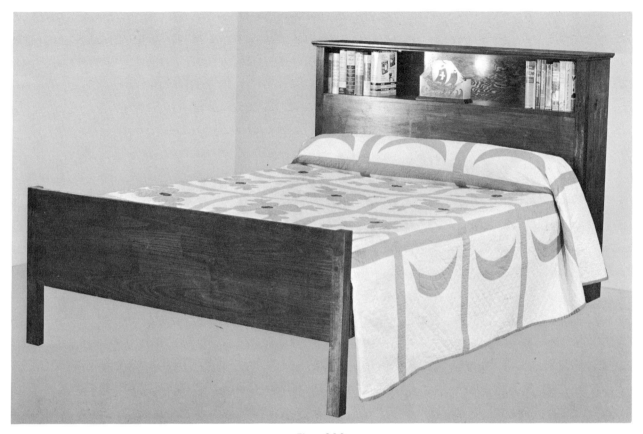

Fig. 220

The lightweight modern type bed shown in Figure 220 is attractive in appearance and quite easy to build. No difficult construction is involved. The bed takes standard double-bed-sized box springs and mattress. Easily obtainable gray iron castings are used to join rails to head and foot posts, as shown in Figures 221 and 222.

The bookshelf is an aesthetic as well as a practical improvement over the usual plain headboard variety of bedsteads. The wood used here was yellow poplar.

To make the bed, first square the posts. Groove the headboard posts, both for the ends, which are tongued on the front edges, then glued to the posts, and for the headboard, which is fastened under the bookshelf in the same manner. Also rab-

bet the rear edges of the ends at the top, to which the plywood back of the bookshelf will later be nailed. Cut notches in posts for the brace strip at the back, as shown in Figure 222.

### BILL OF MATERIAL

| DESCRIPTION | PIECES | DIMENSIONS |
|---|---|---|
| Posts on head of bed | 2 | 1¾ x 1¾ x 42¼ |
| Posts on foot of bed | 2 | 1¾ x 1¾ x 23½ |
| Ends of head of bed | 2 | ¾ x 8⅞ x 42¼ |
| Shelf in head of bed | 1 | ¾ x 10 x 54 |
| Top of head of bed | 1 | ¾ x 11 x 57 |
| Headboard | 1 | ¾ x 22 x 52¾ |
| Footboard | 1 | ¾ x 14 x 52¾ |
| Rails | 2 | ¾ x 7 x 75 |
| Strips on inside of rails | 2 | ¾ x 1¾ x 75 |
| Brace strip on back of head | 1 | ¾ x 2 x 55½ |
| Slats | 6 | ¾ x 2 x 54 |
| Back, for bookshelf (plywood) | 1 | ¼ x 11⅛ x 54¾ |

105

# Bed

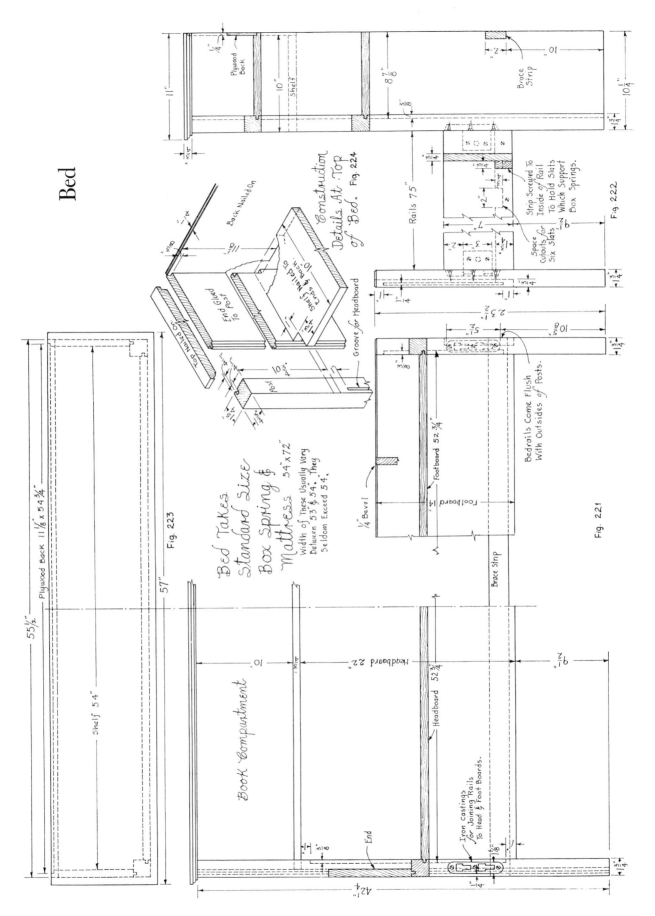

Construction Details At Top of Bed. Fig. 224

Rails 75"

Strip Screwed To Inside of Rail To Hold Slats Which Support Box Springs.

Space Cutouts for Six Slats

Fig. 222

Back Nailed On

End Glued To Post

Shelf Nailed To Ends & Back

Groove for Headboard

Post

Bed Takes Standard Size Box Spring & Mattress 54"x72"

Width of These Usually Vary Between 53 & 54". They Seldom Exceed 54".

Fig. 223

Plywood Back 11 1/8 x 54 3/4"

Shelf 54"

Book Compartment

End

Headboard 22"

Headboard 52 3/4"

Iron Castings for Joining Rails To Head & Foot Boards.

Brace Strip

¼ Bevel

Footboard 52 3/4"

Footboard 14"

Bedrails Come Flush With Outsides of Posts.

Fig. 221

Plywood Back

Shelf

Brace Strip

Before assembling the parts comprising the head of the bed, mortise out for the iron castings, and fasten the castings flush with the front faces of the posts, as shown in Figures 221 and 222. Foot posts and footboard are treated in much the same manner, and then glued together.

Make the rails, and fasten the castings which join the head and foot of the bed together. Further details of construction of the head of the bed are given in Figure 224.

Strips the same length as the rails, after being notched for slats, are screwed fast to the inside of the rails. Besides acting as supporting members for the slats, these make the rails more rigid.

A molding is cut on the underside of the top of the head of the bed, as shown in the drawings.

# 33. Early Colonial Chest of Drawers

The amply proportioned chest of drawers shown in Figure 225 will fit into almost any Colonial or traditional setting, and it has the simplicity of design and surface ornament which would fit it into a contemporary setting as well. In place of surface decoration, its beauty is dependent upon other factors, such as good proportions, simplicity of outline, and the natural beauty of the wood grain enhanced by the transparency of the finish.

The ends are made first. Frames which support and separate the drawers are made next. After rabbeting the rear edges of the ends, the frames are fastened to the ends with wood screws from the inside, as shown in Figure 228. When the

Fig. 225

## BILL OF MATERIAL

| DESCRIPTION | PRICES | DIMENSIONS |
|---|---|---|
| Ends (A) | 2 | ¾ x 19¼ x 42¼ |
| Stiles on front (B) | 2 | ¾ x 1⅝ x 42¼ |
| Front rails of frames (C) | 5 | 1³⁄₁₆ x 2 x 38½ |
| | | (See Fig. 228.) |
| Rear rails of frames (D) | 5 | 1³⁄₁₆ x 1½ x 38½ |
| End rails of frames (E) | 10 | 1³⁄₁₆ x 2 x 18⅝ |
| Middle rails of frames (F) | 5 | 1³⁄₁₆ x 2½ x 18⅝ |
| Center runs on frames (G) | 4 | ⅜ x 1 x 18⅞ |
| Grooved center run guide strips (H) | 4 | ½ x 2½ x 18⅞ |
| Front of base (I) | 1 | ¾ x 4¾ x 41½ |
| Ends of base (J) | 2 | ¾ x 4¾ x 20¾ |
| Rear of base (K) | 1 | ¾ x 4¾ x 38½ |
| Top (L) | 1 | ¾ x 20¾ x 41½ |
| Upper drawer front (M) | 1 | 1³⁄₁₆ x 5⁵⁄₁₆ x 36¹¹⁄₁₆ |
| Second drawer front (N) | 1 | 1³⁄₁₆ x 7⁵⁄₁₆ x 36¹¹⁄₁₆ |
| Third drawer front (O) | 1 | 1³⁄₁₆ x 8⁵⁄₁₆ x 36¹¹⁄₁₆ |
| Lower drawer front (P) | 1 | 1³⁄₁₆ x 10¹⁵⁄₁₆ x 36¹¹⁄₁₆ |
| Upper drawer sides (Q) | 2 | ⅝ x 5¹⁵⁄₁₆ x 19⅝ |
| Second drawer sides (R) | 2 | ⅝ x 7¹⁵⁄₁₆ x 19⅝ |
| Third drawer sides (S) | 2 | ⅝ x 8¹⁵⁄₁₆ x 19⅝ |
| Lower drawer sides (T) | 2 | ⅝ x 10¹⁵⁄₁₆ x 19⅝ |
| Upper drawer back (U) (plywood) | 1 | ⅜ x 5⁵⁄₁₆ x 35¹⁵⁄₁₆ |
| Second drawer back (plywood) (V) | 1 | ⅜ x 7⁵⁄₁₆ x 35¹⁵⁄₁₆ |
| Third drawer back (plywood) (W) | 1 | ⅜ x 8⁵⁄₁₆ x 35¹⁵⁄₁₆ |
| Lower drawer back (plywood) (X) | 1 | ⅜ x 10⅝ x 35¹⁵⁄₁₆ |
| Drawer bottoms (plywood) (Y) | 4 | ⅜ x 19⅝ x 35¹⁵⁄₁₆ |
| Back of chest (plywood) (Z) | 1 | ⅜ x 38⁷⁄₁₆ x 39¼ |

frames are in place, the top is made and screwed fast to the frame, as shown in Figure 227.

Cut out and nail on the back. Next, cut out and screw fast the two stiles (B), which are the front posts of the chest. Holes are counterbored for the wood screws which are used to fasten the stiles to the chest. These holes are then plugged to hide the screwheads. The plugs are decorative as well as functional.

With a shaper, cut molding on the upper edges of the base, and fasten this to the chest with 4-penny finishing nails. A reinforcing strip, like the one shown in Figure 226, will help to hold the front of the base more securely.

Drawers on a fine chest such as this one should if possible be made with blind dovetail joints, as shown in Figure 231. However, an equally strong joint, like the type shown in Figure 232, which can be more quickly made on the variety or circular saw, will, of course, serve the purpose. Yellow poplar was the wood used to make this chest.

# Early Colonial Chest of Drawers

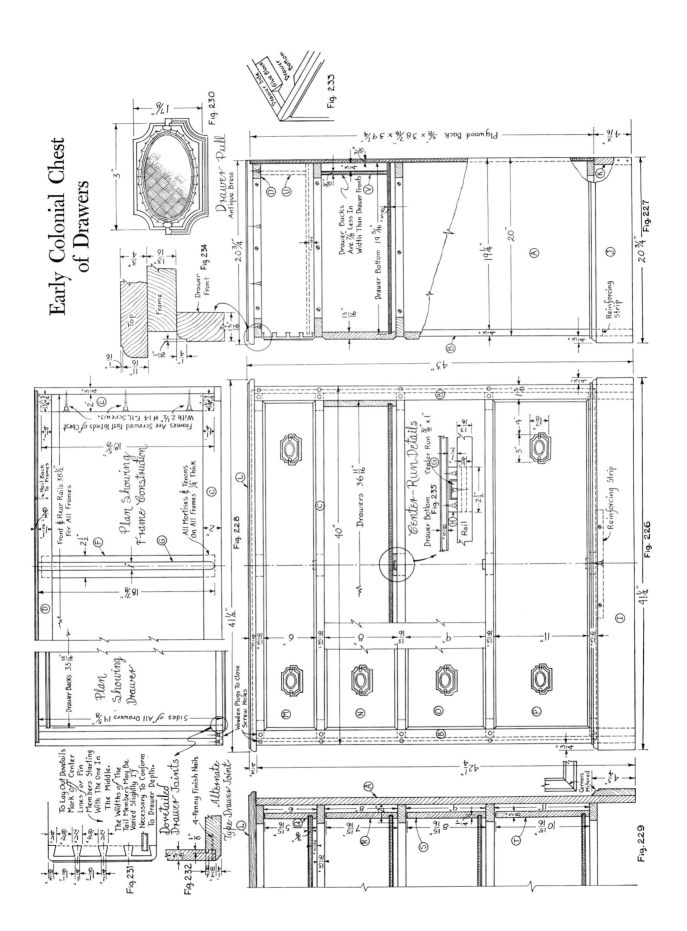

# 34.  Chest of Drawers

The chest of drawers shown in Figure 236 is taller and narrower than the one described in the previous chapter. It is also a type which must be identified with an earlier furniture period. It is tall and rather narrow in width and depth, and will, therefore, occupy a smaller floor area, and yet still provide a considerable amount of storage area. The chest illustrated was built of yellow pine.

To build it, first make the ends. Cut out the shape for the feet, and rabbet the rear edges for the back.

Fig. 236

## BILL OF MATERIAL

| DESCRIPTION | PIECES | DIMENSIONS |
|---|---|---|
| Ends (A) | 2 | ¾ x 17¼ x 41 |
| Posts on front (B) | 2 | ¾ x 2 x 41 |
| Rail at bottom (C) | 1 | ¾ x 2 x 28 |
| Front rails, upper five frames (D) | 5 | ¾ x 2 x 28 |
| Front rail, lower frame (E) | 1 | ¾ x 1¼ x 28 |
| Back rails, all frames (F) | 6 | ¾ x 2 x 28 |
| End and center rails, all frames (G) | 17 | ¾ x 2 x 16⅝ |
| Center runs (H) | 5 | ⅜ x 1 x 17⅛ |
| Tracks for center runs (I) | 5 | ½ x 2½ x 17⅛ |
| Upper drawer front (J) | 1 | ¾ x 4¾ x 26 |
| Second drawer front (K) | 1 | ¾ x 6 x 26 |
| Three lower drawer fronts (L) | 3 | ¾ x 8 x 26 |
| Upper drawer sides (M) | 2 | ⅝ x 4³⁄₁₆ x 17⅝ |
| Second drawer sides (N) | 2 | ⅝ x 5⁷⁄₁₆ x 17⅝ |
| Sides, three lower drawers (O) | 6 | ⅝ x 7⁷⁄₁₆ x 17⅝ |
| Back, upper drawer (plywood) (P) | 1 | ⅜ x 3⁵⁄₁₆ x 24¹³⁄₁₆ |
| Back, second drawer plywood) (Q) | 1 | ⅜ x 4⁹⁄₁₆ x 24¹³⁄₁₆ |
| Backs, three lower drawers (plywood) (R) | 3 | ⅜ x 6⁹⁄₁₆ x 24¹³⁄₁₆ |
| Drawer bottoms (plywood) (S) | 5 | ⅜ x 17⅜ x 24¹³⁄₁₆ |
| Top of chest (T) | 1 | ¾ x 19 x 32½ |
| Pulls (U) | 10 | 1⅛ x 1¼ |
| Back (plywood) (V) | 1 | ⅜ x 28¾ x 37⅛ |

Make the frames, construction details of which are shown in Figure 240. Note that front corners of the frames are cut away to make room for the posts (B), which are nailed to the ends of the chest with finishing nails and screwed fast to the frames. Frames are screwed fast to the ends. The back of the chest is nailed to the frames and ends with lathing nails.

Make the top, rabbeting the rear edge where the back is to be nailed to it. Screws through the upper frame help to hold the top in place. See Figure 239.

Drawer sides should be dovetailed to fronts as shown in the detail of Figures 238 and 241. The dovetailing on these drawers consists of a pin in the center, one on top and another on the bottom of the drawer fronts, with two tails on each of the sides, as shown in Figure 241. Such dovetail construction is about as simple as it can be made on drawers as deep as these, though more tails and pins may be added if so desired. Another type of drawer joint, like the one shown in Figure 232 in Chapter 33, may be substituted for the dovetail joint if so desired.

Wooden drawer pulls, like the knobs shown in Figure 243, are proper for a chest of so early a style as that from which this one was adapted.

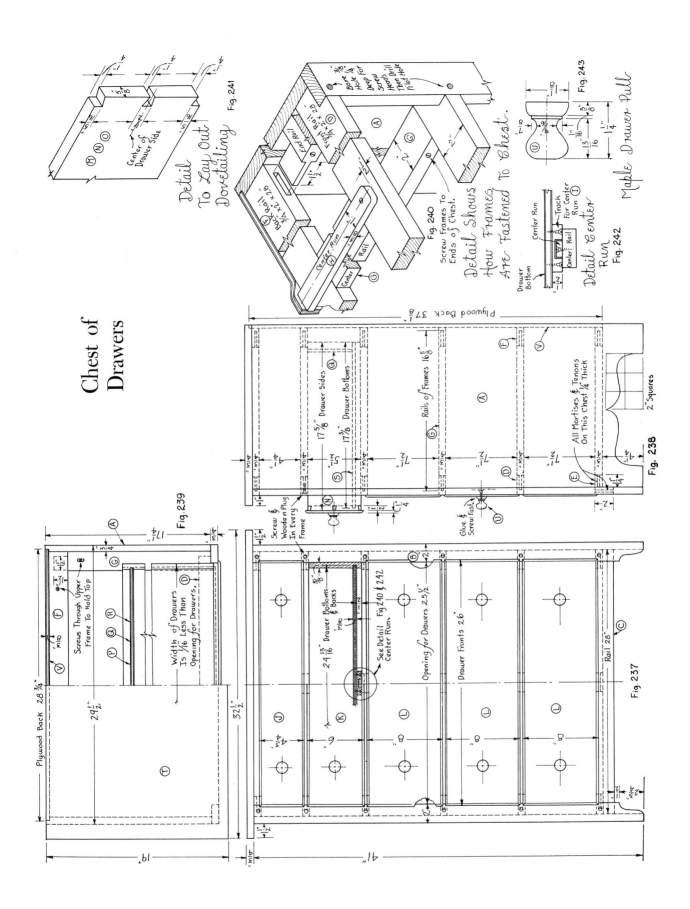

# Chest of Drawers

**Detail To Lay Out Dovetailing** Fig. 241

**Detail Shows How Frames Are Fastened To Chest.** Fig. 240

Screw Frames To Ends of Chest.

Bore ¼ Hole For Screw Heads ⅜" Deep Then Drill Pilot Hole

End Rail

Center Run

Rail

Center Rail

**Maple Drawer Pull** Fig. 243

**Detail Center Run** Fig. 242

Track For Center Run
Center Run
Center Rail
Drawer Bottom

Plywood Back 37⅛"

Fig. 238

17⅝" Drawer Sides
17⅜" Drawer Bottoms
Rails of Frames 16⅝"

All Mortises & Tenons On This Chest ¼ Thick

2" Squares

Screw & Wooden Plug In Every Frame
Glue & Screw Fast

Fig. 239

Plywood Back 28¾"
17¼"
29½"
32½"

Screws Through Upper Frame To Hold Top

Width of Drawers Is 1/16 Less Than Opening for Drawers.

24 13/16 Drawer Bottoms & Backs
Fig. 240 & 242
See Detail Center Run.

Opening for Drawers 2.5½"
Drawer Fronts 26"
Rail 28"
Fig. 237

19"
41"